STUDY GUIDE EDITION

Reading Scripture as the Word of God

Practical Approaches and Attitudes

George Martin

CHARIS

SERVANT PUBLICATIONS
ANN ARBOR, MICHIGAN

Published by Servant Publications
P.O. Box 8617
Ann Arbor, Michigan 48107

Nihil Obstat: Reverend Robert Lunsford
Imprimatur: Most Reverend Alexander Zaleski
          Bishop of Lansing

The *nihil obstat* and i*mprimatur* are official declarations that a book
or pamphlet is free from doctrinal or moral error. No implication is
contained therein that those who grant the *nihil obstat* or *imprimatur* agree with the contents, opinions, or statements expressed.

Scripture quotations in this book are taken from the following trans-
lations and used by permission: The Jerusalem Bible (JB) © 1966
by Darton, Longman & Todd, Ltd. and Doubleday & Company;
The New Revised Standard Version (NRSV) © 1989 by the
Division of Christian Education of the National Council of the
Churches of Christ in the U.S.A.; The New American Bible with
Revised New Testament (NAB) © 1986 by the Confraternity of
Christian Doctrine; and The New English Bible (NEB) © 1970 by
Oxford University Press.

Cover design: Alicia Vazquez

          01 02   10 9 8 7 6 5 4

Printed in the United States of America
ISBN 1-56955-061-1

Library of Congress Cataloging-in-Publication Data

Martin, George, 1939–

    Reading scripture as the word of God : practical approach-
es and attitudes / George Martin.—3rd ed.
    201 p.   cm.
    ISBN 0-89283-152-9
    1. Bible—Study and teaching. I. Title.
BS600.2.M188   1993
220'.07—dc20   93-26978

To Mary, my wife,
and Bert, my friend.

Contents

A Note on Translations of
Scripture Used in This Book

Different translations of Scripture bring out different nuances of meaning in attempting to be faithful to what the authors wrote in Hebrew and Greek. A number of different translations are used in this book. When a Scripture reference is given, the translation is indicated by the following abbreviations:

JB—Jerusalem Bible
NJB—New Jerusalem Bible
NAB—New American Bible
NEB—New English Bible
RSV—Revised Standard Version
NRSV—New Revised Standard Version

The Purpose of This Book

THIS BOOK is about *reading* Scripture, and reading it as God's word addressed to us.

This is a practical book, intended to help those who wish to begin reading Scripture, or want to mature in their understanding of Scripture. It focuses on our using Scripture to grow in the Christian life, and on the way that God addresses his word to us through the words of Scripture.

Part I of this book is on *Reading Scripture*. It provides practical suggestions for reading Scripture, for growing in understanding what we read, for listening to the word of God speak to us through Scripture, and for using Scripture in our prayer. Its purpose is to help Scripture "come alive" for us.

Part II is on *The Word of God*, and is concerned with how God reveals himself to us through the words of Scripture. It discusses how we should approach Scripture as the word of God spoken to us in human words, and how Scripture reveals God himself to us, forming us into his people.

Part III is on *Abiding in the Word*, and takes up topics and questions that arise once we begin reading Scripture. We will have good days and bad days; we will sometimes be baffled by problems of interpretation; we will often experience the power of God's word: all this is a part of remaining faithful to daily reading and abiding in God's word.

This Fourth Edition adds a Postscript and a Study Guide; an earlier version of the Postscript appeared in *New Covenant* magazine. The Third Edition used more gender-neutral language and updated some bibliographic references. The Second Edition of *Reading Scripture as the Word of God* revised and updated the text of the First Edition, and also incorporated some additional material that was first published in the monthly magazine, *God's Word Today*. The basic purpose and plan of the book have remained the same, however, through all editions.

My aim has not been to write an original book, but a usable book. Most of the ideas contained in this book are in such common circulation that it is impossible to acknowledge their sources. If this book has any merit, it is in presenting these ideas in a readable and practical form.

Special gratitude is due, however, to George Montague, S.M., Brian Moore, and Kevin Ranaghan for their advice in writing this work, and to James Manney, Nicholas Cavnar, and Bert Ghezzi for their help in editing it.

I read Scripture and write this book from within the Roman Catholic tradition—but I believe that what I write is true and valid for every Christian who would read Scripture as the Word of God.

Part I

Reading Scripture

ONE

Reading

As the rain and the snow come down from the heavens and do not return without watering the earth, making it yield and giving growth to provide seed for the sower and bread for the eating, so the word that goes from my mouth does not return to me empty, without carrying out my will and succeeding in what it was sent to do.   Isaiah 55:10-11 JB

GOD'S WORD BROKE INTO THE LIFE of Abram nearly four thousand years ago—and a stream of revelation began which reached its fulfillment in Jesus of Nazareth and continues in our hearts today.

God's word bid Abram to leave his country and father's house for a new land. Abram's willing response changed his life, and changed human history: Abram became Abraham, the father of a people that God adopted as his own. Through this chosen people, God continued to speak his word, revealing himself to humankind.

In the fullness of time, God's word came not merely as a message but as a person: the Word of God came as flesh and bone, and lived in our midst. God's Word was not only spoken to us but became one of us, the man named Jesus of Nazareth.

Today we can drink from that same stream of revelation. God reveals himself to us, God adopts us as sons and daughters, God gives us life itself, through his Word spoken to us, Jesus Christ, the Lord.

God sends his word to us as he sent it to Abram: to reveal himself, to transform us, to create for himself a people. His word is not an empty or powerless word: it is a life-giving word, a transforming word.

The word of God is spoken to us in a variety of ways. It is spoken through the Church, the body of Christ. It is spoken to our hearts in prayer. And it is spoken through the words of the Bible.

Reading the Bible as the word of God can allow a power to flow into our lives, a power that can transform us. Listening to the word of God spoken through the words of Scripture can draw us deeper into a relationship with God himself. Scripture becomes a means for the power of God to take hold of us and reshape us, bringing us to fuller life.

Scripture speaks of the power of God's word. "Is not my word like fire, says the Lord, like a hammer shattering rocks?" (Jer 23:29 NAB). "For the word of God is living and active, sharper than any two-edged sword, piercing to the division of soul and spirit, of joints and marrow, and discerning the thoughts and intentions of the heart" (Heb 4:12 RSV). This same powerful word of God is addressed to us to bring us life. It is "the saving power of God for everyone who has faith" (Rom 1:16 NEB); it has "power to build up and to give you your inheritance among all the sanctified" (Acts 20:32 JB).

This book is about reading Scripture as the word of God, about reading it in such a way that God himself can speak his word to us, transforming us, transforming our relationship with him. This book is about listening to the word of God in such a way that his word does not return to him empty, but carries out his will within us.

DAILY READING

The first step in listening to the word of God speak to us through Scripture is to begin reading the Bible, and to begin reading it *daily*.

Too many of us begin to read Scripture with a jackrabbit start and a resolution to read the Bible from cover to cover—but then get tired and distracted and fail to carry out our resolve.

The Bible is a big book, too big to be read simply from a burst of enthusiasm. If we are ever to read it completely, our reading must be sustained by commitment rather than enthusiasm. If we are ever to become immersed in its revelation to us, our reading must become an integral part of our lives, not just an incidental activity that we do now and then.

I believe that the most practical step we can take to read the Bible as God's word to us is to commit ourselves to reading it every day. Our daily reading need not take a lot of time; fifteen minutes is an acceptable initial commitment. But it must be done faithfully, day after day, no matter how we feel or how hectic things are for us. This kind of faithfulness requires commitment, a firm determination that we are going to read the Bible fifteen minutes every day, no matter what.

Such a program of daily reading is the basis for reading Scripture as the word of God. Of course, daily reading is not sufficient in itself. Our reading should be done prayerfully; our understanding of Scripture must be aided by study, making use of the various helps at our disposal. Further, we need some understanding of the role that Scripture plays in God's revelation of himself, and some skill in listening to God speak to us through the words of Scripture. But all our skills in understanding the Bible must begin and end in our actually reading the Bible, so that our lives may be transformed by him who speaks to us through its words.

This vital reading of Scripture should be done daily, as an integral part of our daily spiritual nourishment and of our daily routine. Reading Scripture is not like going out to dinner on special occasions; it must be like the evening supper that families share, day in, day out. Periodic times of intensive reading of the Bible are a good idea, just as occasional evenings out together build a marriage. But just as our daily supper nourishes us, our daily reading of Scripture will bring the strength of God into our everyday lives. Anything less than daily reading is likely to lead to spiritual malnutrition.

The process of our growth into the image of Christ begins

with our baptism into Jesus Christ and will end with the resurrection of our bodies into everlasting union with him. Throughout, God continually calls us to grow in love and discipleship. At all times we must listen to the word of God speaking to us, beckoning us on. Our need to read Scripture to listen to God's voice never ends.

The complexity of Scripture and its inexhaustible depths should not discourage us from beginning to read it. We are not called to read the Bible in order to pass a test at the end of the month, or at the end of a year. The "test" will come at the end of our lives, and then we shall be asked about our love, not about our ability as Scripture scholars. God has given us Scripture precisely to help us meet this "test" of love. We must not be overwhelmed by what we do not know about Scripture; we should be consoled that God has given us Scripture as a means of growing in faith, in hope, in love, in union with him.

We shall grow in union with God as we begin a program of daily reading of Scripture and pursue this program faithfully. We can underestimate the impact of a modest commitment, honored day after day, year after year. The fruit of our daily Scripture reading is something which is better experienced than described —because it is an effect that takes place deep within us.

We marvel at the beauty of the Grand Canyon—a monument created by the Colorado River's slow but persistent erosion of rock, an erosion too slow to be seen except in its fantastic effects.

Something similar can happen to us. We have 1440 minutes to live each day of our lives. If we spend fifteen of those minutes prayerfully listening to the word of God speak to us through the words of the Bible, it will make a difference in the other 1425 minutes. If we spend a few minutes alone with God's word each day, every day, day after day, in the course of our years they will play a significant role in our transformation in Christ.

We should be warned, however, that the Bible is not a book of magic. By itself it cannot change our lives, no matter how much we read it. It can, however, be a means whereby the same Holy Spirit who inspired the authors of the Bible can inspire us—and not only inspire us to understand what we read, but empower us to enter into the reality that we read about. What is sacred for us about sacred Scripture is that through the words of Scripture we can listen to the words of God, and that through listening to and obeying the word of God we can be transformed into his image.

In short, the Bible is not a book to be learned and mastered, like a book of ancient history. Nor is it like a detective novel that we can read once to find out "who dunnit" and set it aside. It is a book that we need to return to each day, rereading familiar passages in order to enter more deeply into the mystery that they reveal.

To enter into this mystery of God's word, your lifetime of listening to the word of God can begin, *today*, with a fifteen-minute reading. If need be, stop reading this book fifteen minutes sooner than you had planned and begin reading the Gospel according to Luke. Then continue this commitment for the rest of your life.

A commitment to read the Bible is not sufficient in itself. We must approach our reading in a certain way; we must expect certain things to happen; we need practical help with Scripture's complexities; we must obey the word of God as we hear it. The rest of this book discusses these and other matters. But we must first *read*, daily and faithfully. Begin today, and continue tomorrow, and the day after that.

KINDS OF READING

The fifteen-minute daily reading of Scripture which provides the backbone of our growth in hearing the word of God should be of a certain type and character. It should be a sustained, reflective reading, alert to both detail and context, which gradually draws us deeper into the mystery of God's revelation in Scripture.

There are other kinds of Scripture reading, each having its own pace and characteristics.

Sometimes it is advisable to rather quickly read a whole book or long section through, to get an overview of it. It is profitable, for instance, to read some of Paul's shorter letters as we would read any letter we receive: reading it through from beginning to end, and then going back through it more slowly a second time. This type of rather quick reading is also appropriate for many parts of the Old Testament, particularly the historical books. A straight-through reading of a long section provides an idea of "the lay of the land"; the more significant passages can be marked for later careful reading and reflection.

At the other end of the scale lies intense meditation on a single verse, or a few verses, from Scripture. Here the object is not to cover ground or read new material, but to understand as fully as possible a single thought, and to reflect on its applications to one's own life. There are many verses in Scripture whose meaning we will not exhaust in a lifetime of reflection.

Between the sustained reading of a long passage or entire books of Scripture and intensive reflection on a few words lies the kind of reading that should form the basis of our daily reading of Scripture. This reading is characterized neither by a desire to cover a certain amount of material, nor by an attempt to milk the last ounce of meaning from every single verse. It is careful reading, with pauses to reflect on the meaning of what is being read. It is slow reading, leisurely reading, reading with attention to detail and nuance. It is reading with a deliberate yet natural pace, that allows us to linger over a single verse or thought before continuing on. This kind of reading is recommended for our daily time with the word of God.

Each type of reading has its usefulness. Careful daily reading is the foundation of our listening to the word of God speak to us through Scripture. The more rapid reading of whole books should be a part of our Scripture study, and the peaceful reflection on a few words or verses a part of our daily prayer.

Why is fifteen minutes a day recommended for our basic reading? Five minutes is too little to really immerse oneself in the word of God; a half an hour is too long for most of us to sustain an alert and prayerful reading of Scripture, at least at the beginning. Of course, if you are receiving special graces from God drawing you to a deep reading of Scripture for a longer period, by all means do so. Schedules are for the sake of reading, not reading for the sake of schedules.

As we grow in our reading of Scripture, fifteen minutes may indeed prove inadequate and more time each day may be needed. The extra time, however, will usually be spent more in prayer than in reading; prayer based on Scripture will be discussed in chapter four. And as we grow in our understanding of the Bible, we will want to spend time occasionally reading an entire book of the Bible at a sitting, or in reading books about the Bible. Other times should be set aside for Scripture study, and more will be said about Scripture study in chapter two. Our first goal, however, should be a daily fifteen minutes of Scripture reading, a time which will grow in prayerfulness and into prayer.

Our reading of Scripture should be done in such a way that the words sink in, that we grasp the meaning not only with our heads, but also with our hearts. This type of reading can be compared to gazing at a great painting, or to reading poetry. The point in looking at a painting is not to give it a quick glance, say "That's a painting of a woman," and pass on. Art must be viewed contemplatively, with attention to both the broad sweeps of color and design, and to the details. So too with reading a poem: poetry is not meant for speed reading, or to be read once and discarded. Poetry is meant to be read slowly and savored, and to be read repeatedly.

God's word must also be read slowly, and savored. We need to understand the broad sweep of the passage we are reading— an event in Christ's life, an argument from Paul, a prophecy from Isaiah. But we also need to be alert to the details, the nuances of meaning. Even the shortest verse in the Bible has depths of meaning: "Jesus wept" (Jn 11:35 RSV).

Above all, we need to ask, "What are the authors trying to tell their readers?" Why did they think it important to include this event from the life of Jesus? What is Paul trying to get across to the Corinthians? What is the point of this prophecy of Isaiah? This demands that we think about what we are reading as we are reading it—and this requires that we read slowly. Our reading should be paced by our understanding, not by our watches.

SOME PRACTICAL CONSIDERATIONS

A few problems will emerge as soon as we resolve to spend fifteen minutes a day reading Scripture. First, and perhaps most urgently, how do we find the time in our busy schedules? Second, which of the many translations of the Bible should we choose for our reading? Finally, where do we begin? These problems will not afflict everyone equally. Some people's schedules are busier than others; many have long since decided on a favorite translation of the Bible; many have already begun daily reading. Nevertheless, these practical issues are important ones, and need to be discussed.

Finding *the* time. The most common obstacle to daily Scripture reading is not finding the time, but finding *the* time. We all have plenty of time—in the sense that none of us have lives so fully scheduled that we do not have at least fifteen free minutes each day. However, many have trouble finding the right fifteen minutes to be alone with God and his word.

Some people wake up so groggy in the morning that it's almost noontime before their brains are sufficiently clear to undertake anything as important as reading God's word. But by noon, the cares of the day have descended in force, and distractions pile on distractions. In the evening, fatigue may seem to prohibit anything more strenuous than passively watching television.

I suspect that most of us could come up with a list of reasons why there is no suitable fifteen-minute period at any time in our day for reading Scripture. Perhaps the thing to do is to make such a list—and then pick a definite time anyway. We can admit that no time is perfect; but then firmly resolve to set aside fifteen minutes anyway! Not a vague fifteen minutes "sometime," but a definite fifteen minutes at a definite time.

For those who can wake up with some ease (or learn how to), the first minutes in the morning should be the most peaceful and free from distractions. Don't think about all the things that have to be done that day. Simply turn to the Lord, and then turn to your bookmark in the Bible and begin reading.

Others may find the quiet of the evening an ideal time to

place themselves in the presence of the Lord and listen to his word. After the children are in bed and the evening's dishes dried, or after the day's classes have been taught and tests corrected, or after the day's work is done and rush hour traffic survived once more—then we may find the freedom from pressure which will allow us to turn wholeheartedly to God and listen to him without distraction.

Still others will find other times during their days when fifteen minutes can be set aside. It may be at the kitchen table after children go to school and before housework and shopping. It may be at one's desk during the first or last fifteen minutes of lunch hour. It may be the afternoon coffee break at the plant. It may be a fifteen-minute visit to a nearby church during the hour between morning classes. *Everyone* can find the time.

What is important is that we make the time, and that it be a time when our minds are sufficiently alert and free to use the time profitably. For most of us, a vague resolve to spend fifteen minutes "sometime during the day" reading Scripture is unrealistic: sometimes we will, and sometimes we won't. A definite time each day is much to be preferred.

Choosing a translation. To read Scripture with understanding, we need a good translation—and preferably several good translations. Since no translation is perfect, it is desirable to have several at one's disposal.

The first requirement in a translation is accuracy: the faithful rendering of the precise meaning of the original Hebrew and Greek texts. The second requirement is that the meaning of the original be conveyed in fluent and readable English. Fulfilling both requirements is no small task—and many modern translations are the product of committees of scholars and years of work.

It is hard to detect much difference in modern translations of Scripture based on church denominations. We appear to be at the end of the era when "Catholic" and "Protestant" translations vied with each other. The translations being done today are generally based on a scholarship that cuts across denominational lines. Certain translations may be labeled "Catholic" or

"Protestant" largely on the basis of whether they include or omit those books of the Old Testament which Catholics hold to be a part of Scripture but which Protestants consider "apocryphal." However, some "Protestant" translations (such as the RSV) are available in editions which include all the books Catholics consider to be inspired.

The *Revised Standard Version* (RSV) was completed in 1952. It is a revision of the earlier *American Standard* and *King James* versions, but a revision in light of the Hebrew and Greek manuscripts. The RSV seeks to preserve its literary heritage from the earlier translations, and is usually characterized by scholars as both a literal and a literate translation. The RSV is one of the most widely used translations available, and overall is entirely adequate and useful. A revision of the RSV (NRSV) was published in 1989.

The *Jerusalem Bible* (JB) appeared in English in 1966. It is based on a French counterpart completed some ten years earlier. In general, the JB is a translation from the original languages, but it is written with an eye to the interpretations of the French translators. The introductions to the various books and the notes are basically translations of the introductions and notes from the French edition. The translation is quite fluent and lucid. A revision of the JB (NJB) was published in 1991.

Also appearing in 1966 was *Good News for Modern Man: The New Testament in Today's English Version* (TEV). Since then, editions have appeared which include the Old Testament. The style of TEV is such that anyone who can read a newspaper can understand it; strange words or phrases are kept to a minimum, and those are explained in a word list. While being very readable, this translation seems to be also generally reliable.

Two more translations of the Bible were completed in 1970: *The New English Bible* (NEB) and *The New American Bible* (NAB). Both are "fresh" translations from the original languages, rather than revisions of previous translations. The NEB was done in England, and in places reads "British" rather than "American." Its general accuracy and reliability, however, are entirely adequate.

The New American Bible (NAB) was translated by members of the Catholic Biblical Association of America, and was highly acclaimed at the time of its publication. This translation is both accurate and readable, and reflects the latest scholarship. A revised translation of the New Testament was completed and published in 1986 (NAB with Revised New Testament) and a revised translation of the Old Testament is currently underway. The NAB translation is used in the liturgy of the Catholic Church.

One other modern version may be mentioned: *The Living Bible,* published by Tyndale House in 1971. This is not a translation but a paraphrase. While it is very readable, it is not as literally faithful to the original languages as the translations mentioned above. It has sold millions of copies since its publication, and has introduced countless readers to Scripture. However, I believe it is more desirable to wrestle with the difficulties of an accurate translation than to rely on a paraphrase of what the sacred authors said—however much more readable the paraphrase might be.

In summary, the RSV, JB, TEV, NAB, and NEB are all adequate for use in spiritual reading and study including the NRSV, the NJB, and the NAB with revised New Testament. Scholars can fault each of them for certain lapses—but for those who cannot read Greek and Hebrew, they may be taken as reliable translations into understandable English.

Many people have other translations in their homes—and perhaps have had them for years. Unless they are both accurate and readable translations, it would be best to set them aside and buy one of the above translations for daily use.

The traditional Protestant and Catholic translations, the *King James Version* and the *Douay-Rheims Version,* were prized translations in their time, and the *King James Version* is a literary masterpiece. But in the three hundred years since they appeared, Scripture scholarship has made significant advances. Modern translations are based on a more accurate Hebrew and Greek text than was available in the seventeenth century. Equally important, the English language has changed since the *King*

James and *Douay-Rheims* translations were made. Literally hundreds of words have a different meaning today than they did then; the language and meaning of these older translations is often obscure to us today.

There is value in consistently reading one translation of Scripture and allowing its phrasing of key passages to become familiar, almost to the point of unconscious memorization. An important part of our understanding of Scripture comes when we read one passage but hear echoes of others—when we sense a Gospel reference to the Servant Songs of Isaiah without having to check cross references in the margins. To have read and reread and meditated on one translation allows its phrasing and cadences to sink into our minds, and makes further reading all the more fruitful.

At the same time, other translations will bring out different nuances in familiar passages, and provide us with fresh insights. While we might rely mainly on one translation, I cannot recommend relying *solely* on one translation. A second and perhaps third translation should be kept close at hand and referred to in the course of our study of Scripture.

Poetry is particularly hard to translate from one language to another, and the portions of Scripture that are poetic are hence among the most difficult portions to translate. This is particularly true for the Psalms, which rely on poetic constructions and imagery to convey their meaning. A literal translation of a psalm can sound very clumsy to our ears and deprive us of the meaningful prayer that the original conveyed.

It is therefore advisable to consult different translations of Scripture in order to gain an appreciation of the full meaning of the original text. This is particularly important when we are studying a key passage of Scripture and meditating on its meaning; for example, the marks of love listed by Paul in 1 Corinthians 13:4-7. Reading how different translations convey the imagery of the Psalms can likewise be very helpful to us.

I would urge making an investment in a high quality edition of the Bible, complete with notes and introductions, and purchasing a second translation of the New Testament for comparative purposes. My own personal preference is the *New American Bible with Revised New Testament*. One of the many inexpensive editions of the *New Revised Standard Version* New Testament could be used for comparison purposes.

Finally, we should be warned against searching for *the* perfect translation, *the* perfect unambiguous rendering of every passage in Scripture, *the* undisputed meaning of every text. We must realize that any translation is just that: a translation. No translation is perfect; no translation is sacred—even of sacred Scripture. A phrase from another language may often be accurately translated in more than one way. Scholars have been translating the Scriptures since Alexandrian Jews put the Old Testament into Greek around 200 B.C. New translations will undoubtedly continue to appear, each trying to render more accurately the languages of Scripture into our own.

Where to begin. For someone approaching the Bible for the first time, it would be a bad idea to begin with the first chapter and first verse of the Book of Genesis, and plan on reading the Bible straight through to the last verse of the last chapter of the Book of Revelation. Contrary to what we may expect, the books of the Bible do not appear in the order they were written, nor even in the historical order of the events they describe. There is no particular advantage to beginning our Scripture reading with Genesis, and several disadvantages. Most likely we will bog down somewhere in the laws of Leviticus or the genealogies of Numbers, get discouraged, and abandon our reading.

Rather, since we read Scripture as followers of Christ and members of his Church, I would recommend reading first the two works by Luke in the New Testament: the Gospel according to Luke and the Acts of the Apostles. These two books of the New Testament can be read as a two-volume work in themselves, telling us of the good news of Jesus Christ and of the formation of his Church by the Holy Spirit.

Alternately, the Gospel according to Mark could provide a good beginning point, with Paul's letters to the Thessalonians and Corinthians the second stage. John's Gospel and his first letter must be ranked at or near the summit of New Testament revelation, but require very attentive reading. Paul's letters to the Romans and Galatians contain his most profound reflections on the mystery of redemption through Jesus Christ, and demand careful study. The Book of Revelation should probably be the last book of the New Testament to be approached. It cannot be simply read; it must be studied (with the help of a suitable commentary or other aid) if it is to be at all understood. But Luke or Mark make a good starting point.

The vastness of the Old Testament should not inhibit us. Selective reading is more appropriate here: lists of genealogies and pages of dietary laws may well be skimmed or skipped on first reading. The first five books of the Old Testament constitute the basis of God's covenant with his chosen people, and of those, Exodus (not Genesis) should be read first. The historical books (especially Joshua, Judges, the Books of Samuel and Kings) provide the background for understanding the books of the prophets. And they in turn—especially the Book of Isaiah—provide background necessary for truly understanding the New Testament. The other books of the Old Testament, books that contain wisdom, proverbs, prayers, and national stories of the Israelites, may be read within this basic framework.

In reading the Old Testament, some kind of study aid is almost essential. Using an edition of the Bible with good introductions and notes for the various books of Scripture can make a big difference—the notes and study aids in the *Jerusalem Bible* are particularly good. More will be said about growing in our understanding of Scripture and about study aids in the next chapter.

Finally, there is a monthly magazine, *God's Word Today,* which offers Catholics a daily reading guide to the Bible. Edited with the help of the author of this book and published by *Catholic Digest, God's Word Today* focuses on one book of the Bible or one theme from Scripture each month. Over a period of time the various books of the Bible and more important themes of Scripture are studied. The heart of each issue of *God's Word*

Today is a "Daily Reading Guide" which assigns a Scripture reading for each day of the month, and provides a short commentary to help explain that reading and apply it to our Christian lives today. There are also aids for reflection and prayer, as well as practical articles and articles which explore the Bible in more depth. *God's Word Today* provides an answer to the question of where to begin, as well as the daily encouragement and help needed to keep going. An introductory subscription of twelve monthly issues is $14.95: write to *God's Word Today,* PO Box 56915, Boulder, CO 80322-6915.

PRAYER BEFORE READING

Perhaps the most important of the "practical" steps toward reading Scripture as the word of God is to always preface our reading with prayer. It need not be lengthy prayer; in its simplest form, we can merely pray and ask, "Lord, speak to me." But we do need to turn our hearts and minds to God. Our reading of Scripture is not reading for the sake of reading. It is rather reading for the sake of listening to him who loves us.

We can best begin that listening by turning to him—much as we turn toward another person who is talking to us, and to whom we wish to talk. When we listen to someone, we first of all have to pay attention to him or her, and not to whatever else may be going on around us. It is impolite as well as distracting to try to watch television or read the newspaper while carrying on a conversation. So too with our reading of Scripture: we should first turn our attention to God whom we wish to hear. We must tune out all else, not for the sake of "rejecting the world" but simply as a matter of expediency; we can usually only do one thing at a time.

A simple act of turning our minds and hearts to God is the beginning of all prayer, and must likewise be the beginning of our reading Scripture as the word of God. This may take some time. If we are particularly distracted by cares and concerns, we may have to sit quietly for a few minutes, relaxing, putting distractions out of our minds. It is a proper and necessary thing to take our cares and concerns to the Lord in prayer—but not in a way that prevents us from praying, or from listening to him.

Sometimes it is helpful to hold our Bible in our hands for a moment before opening it, and remind ourselves that this book does contain God's word to us: "I am about to read Scripture. I am about to read God's word to me. I want to pay full attention to what I read. I am going to revere the word that I read and try to make it a part of my life."

Our prayer before reading should ask two things of God. First, we should pray that the same Holy Spirit that guided the writing of Scripture will be present in us, inspiring us to correctly understand what we read, and to understand it in ever-increasing depth. As the Second Vatican Council wrote, in reading Scripture "the help of the Holy Spirit must precede and assist, moving the heart and turning it to God, opening the eyes of the mind and giving joy and ease in assenting to the truth and believing it" ("Divine Revelation," section 5).

Secondly, our prayer should ask that we will be empowered to make what we read a part of our lives. In James' phrase, we must "do what the word tells you, and not just listen to it" (Jas 1:22 JB). To obey as well as to understand requires the power of the Holy Spirit in us—and so too should be a matter of our prayer.

If we fully understand what we are praying, we can pray simply, "Lord, speak to me." These simple words can express our turning our minds and hearts to him, our eagerness to understand his word through the presence of his Spirit within us, and to resolve to be formed by his word, conforming our lives to what he asks and offers.

Such prayer should precede our every reading of the Bible. For we do not approach the Bible as we approach any other book. We approach it as an opportunity to listen to him who speaks to us through the words of Scripture. Through the Bible, we approach God himself, and our attitude must be one of prayer.

FAITHFULNESS AND HUMILITY

It is easy to resolve to read the Bible daily; it can be difficult to remain faithful to our resolution. Some of us are blessed with predictable daily schedules that allow us ample quiet time; most of us are not. Most of us, in fact, probably have difficulty finding a regular time when we will not be disturbed and when we are sufficiently free from distractions to be able to read Scripture with the full attention it deserves.

What should we do in the face of such difficulty, a difficulty which tempts us to believe that we will never be able to be very faithful to daily Scripture reading? One answer lies in choosing the best time that is available to us, and safeguarding it. But equally important can be our attitude toward achieving daily Scripture reading in our lives, and the way we cope with our failure to do so.

Put simply, most of us quit too easily. We fall, and pick ourselves up, and fall again. After four or five falls, we give up the struggle thinking that we are doomed to fail forever. Rather than struggle after an ideal that continually seems to elude us, we lower our ideals and our expectations of ourselves until they match where we are. If we haven't been able to make daily Scripture reading a part of our lives after a few weeks or months, we assume we will never be able to do it, and give up the effort.

At least in my own life I find that change comes exceedingly slowly and gradually. I don't know that I have ever been able to change myself or my behavior immediately, simply because I decided that it was right to do so. Whatever changes or growth have taken place in me have come only after sustained effort and prayer.

To make daily Scripture reading a part of our lives may take a sustained effort for some of us. If we are committed to staying with our resolve, no matter how often we fail, then we can be a little more patient with ourselves when we fail. We didn't expect to remake ourselves instantly, and sure enough, we haven't. But we are still trying, and with God's grace we will succeed.

Sometimes in our reading of Scripture, the print will seem to leap off the page at us, full of meaning for our lives. Reading Scripture is then a pure joy, and we may have trouble tearing ourselves away from it. Yet at other times not only will the print fail to leap off the page, but it will seem to blur before our eyes. Our reading can then be decidedly dry, uninspiring, and burdensome. Our minds will wander despite our best effort to concentrate, and we may be very tempted to give up the whole enterprise.

We should hope and pray to receive the grace of Scripture being "alive" for us. And there are ways of reading that can help in making it come alive; some of these will be discussed in chapter three. But it would be most unwise to give up reading Scripture because it seems to be dry and unrewarding. We can learn much and profit greatly even on those days when nothing *seems* to be happening as we read. As in the rest of the Christian life, "if we do not relax our efforts, in due time we shall reap our harvest" (Gal 6:9 NAB). If athletes only worked out when they "really felt like it," they would never get in good enough shape to win. They would never, in fact, get in good enough shape to ever enjoy working out.

Sometimes our problems of dryness may stem from a seeming overfamiliarity with a given passage. We can read the first few words of a familiar parable, and find that our minds jump through the entire parable to the end. Our eyes may continue reading, but our minds have wandered off somewhere else. Even though a passage may be familiar, we should realize that it contains more depth of meaning than we already understand. In a very real sense, we can always approach the words of Scripture, even very familiar words, expecting to understand them more deeply.

As we continue in our reading of the Bible, even very familiar parts will take on new meaning. The Bible helps explain itself: greater familiarity with the whole of Scripture provides a greater understanding of its individual books and passages. For example, the title "Lamb of God," which John the Baptist uses to introduce Jesus, is undoubtedly familiar to us. But until we have read enough of the Old Testament to catch the double resonance of the Passover lamb of Exodus and of Isaiah's "servant" lamb that is led to the slaughter, we will fail to catch the deepest significance of John the Baptist's reference.

We should also seek to better understand how familiar passages apply to our lives. As our lives change, Scripture's meaning for us will change. When we read as children, we understood as children. As we grow, our understanding grows—not only in the sense that we are now capable of greater intellectual feats, but in the sense that our greater life experience equips us to plumb the greater depths of God's word. As we enter more fully into the mystery of Jesus Christ, his words to us take on greater meaning. The more deeply we plunge into the Christian mystery and into Scripture, the more we see that this mystery is inexhaustible, and that Scripture possesses depths still to be plumbed.

Sometimes the words of Scripture will seem lifeless not because they are so familiar, but because they are so obscure. Portions of the Book of Revelation will most likely strike us as very strange. Or the obscurity may lie not in the book itself but in its meaning for us. For example, we may utterly fail to see the relevance to our own lives of the bloody wars of the Old Testament. Similarly, the words of a long genealogy will seldom "leap from the page."

The best strategy in such cases is simply to peacefully pass over what is obscure, or what seems to lack relevance to one's Christian life today. Often when we reread these same passages a year later, they will take on meaning for us. But rather than focus now on what we do not appreciate or understand, we should focus on what does have a meaning for us. We cannot expect to become knowledgeable of the whole of Scripture all at once. As our reading continues, our understanding will grow, and difficult passages will begin to take on life.

This is not to say that we should not make a serious attempt to understand what we read. Nor does it mean that we should be quick to discard portions of Scripture as unimportant. Rather our attitude must be one of humility: recognizing that we have a long way to go in understanding the Bible, patiently pursuing our reading of it. If the aim of our reading is to listen to the Word of God speak to us, then what is of primary importance for us are those portions of the Bible that his Holy Spirit does make clear to us. Our goal should be to have an understanding of the whole of the Bible and all its books—but this is a goal which we should pursue with patience and perseverance. Above all, we should not lose sight of the basic reason we are reading Scripture in the first place: we are not trying to become an expert about a book, but to listen to the word of God speaking to us.

Our reading can also become sidetracked by questions or disputes about the meaning of certain passages. Perhaps we have heard someone claim that none of the miracles reported in the Bible ever happened—that they are all pious fiction. Or we may have encountered someone of just the opposite view, who believes in the literal truth of *every* word in the Bible. We can probably sort out the more extreme views and reject them. But what are we to do about the many difficult passages in Scripture, and how do we sort out the many different interpretations which have been given to them?

We should not become distracted by questions that we cannot answer, or issues that we cannot solve. A healthy dose of humility is the safest course; to admit that we do not have the final answer, to admit that we simply do not know the answers to all questions. We should persevere in our reading despite what we do not know. We can take comfort in the fact that many disputes over different interpretations of the Bible deal with issues that have little real bearing on our lives.

Still, there are questions whose answers are important, and do bear on what we should believe and how we should live. There will be questions occurring to us as we read the Bible whose answers we should pursue. Proper study of the Bible and about the Bible is indispensable for proper reading of the Bible. We cannot read Scripture as the word of God unless we take his word seriously enough to study it. And this is the subject of the next chapter.

TWO

Understanding

An Ethiopian had been on pilgrimage to Jerusalem; he was a eunuch and an officer of the court of the kandake, or queen, of Ethiopia, and was in fact her chief treasurer. He was now on his way home; and as he sat in his chariot he was reading the prophet Isaiah. The Spirit said to Philip, "Go up and meet that chariot." When Philip ran up, he heard him reading Isaiah the prophet and asked, "Do you understand what you are reading?" "How can I," he replied, "unless I have someone to guide me?" So he invited Philip to get in and sit by his side. Acts 8:27-31 JB

H OW OFTEN HAVE WE FELT like this Ethiopian as we read Scripture? Our hearts are open, our minds alert, our motives sure—yet somehow the meaning of the words eludes us. We read and reread a passage, and still the meaning does not come clear. We wish we had Philip by our side to guide our reading, to give deeper understanding, to answer our questions, and to interpret obscure passages.

The Ethiopian does not appear to be the kind of person who would need help in understanding Scripture. As an important court official, he was intelligent and well educated. He could read Hebrew or Greek as well as his native language. His pilgrimage to Jerusalem indicates that he was a God-fearing man, and recognized a special presence of God in the Jewish people.

Furthermore, the Ethiopian was devoted enough to read Scripture even under difficult circumstances. He was studying Isaiah on a rough road in a chariot that lacked any kind of spring suspension. His reading Scripture despite these handicaps of travel suggests that he was seriously interested in learning its meaning. Even so, he did not understand what he was reading, and needed Philip's assistance.

Luke presents this episode as if it can be taken for granted that the words of Scripture are often difficult to understand. He presents the Ethiopian as a willing reader, but one who needs help to make sense out of the Book of Isaiah.

We should note how the Holy Spirit sent help. He did not choose to directly enlighten the mind of the Ethiopian, but worked through a very "natural" means: Philip. While Philip's appearance on the scene had its miraculous element, the help he gave the Ethiopian was not miraculous. Philip was simply one human being helping another human being understand Scripture. The Ethiopian received no blinding flashes of revelation from the sky—just a providentially arranged hitchhiker who could explain the meaning of Isaiah.

The Holy Spirit continues to work today through the same "natural" means. Sometimes we can detect his hand in providence, arranging circumstances for our benefit. Often we are acutely aware of his presence as we read Scripture and pray. But he will generally use various "natural" guides and means to help us understand the words of Scripture. We will quite rarely receive direct revelations to answer our questions and explain obscure passages. The Holy Spirit plays a role in our reading of Scripture, but so does our own effort.

The problems we face in understanding the Bible are much like the Ethiopian's. Some books of the Bible are quite complex in themselves. But we also can see in the example of the Ethiopian another type of difficulty. Although he was intelligent and dedicated, the Ethiopian was trying to understand a text from a language and a culture that were not his own. It is hard for anyone to cross cultural and language lines and fully understand nuances of meaning. Even an Anglo-American fluent in Spanish cannot simply enter into the culture of Mexico and immediately appreciate its national literature.

The problem is even more severe in reading the Bible. The contrast between our world and the world of Scripture is even greater than that between the United States and Mexico. The Bible comes from a culture other than our own, from an age long past, in languages we do not know. Good translations can bridge the language gap for us—to a point. But the "culture gap" can prove to be a most troublesome problem, even if it is a subtle one. We cannot ignore the specific culture and people God chose to reveal himself in and through. On the contrary, our understanding of that culture and those people is vital to understanding God's words.

In other words, we need to study the Bible if we are to understand its depths of meaning and be able to listen to the word of God speak to us through it. It can be a "hard saying" for us to be told that our study of the Bible must play a role in unlocking the Scripture's personal meaning for us, but that is the case. We cannot hope to understand Scripture unless we face the need to study it.

WHY STUDY?

It is not always obvious that the Bible is a book that must be *studied*. If the Bible is the word of God, shouldn't we expect it to speak to us quite clearly? Shouldn't God address himself equally to the learned and the unlearned, to the scholar and to the ordinary reader? If this is so, why study the Bible, or study about the Bible, when our task should simply be to read it and obey?

A legitimate concern lies behind those questions. Our reading of the Bible must never become merely a scholarly study. God does not judge us on the basis of our intelligence or schooling, but on the basis of our faith and love. At the same time, however, we can use those questions to imply that any study of Scripture is either unnecessary or unwise: unnecessary because God will speak to us whether or not we make an effort to understand Scripture better; unwise because we may confuse ourselves with "human wisdom" and fail to understand God's wisdom for us.

Over the centuries, Christians have taken different views about the complexity of Scripture and the need for study to achieve understanding. One extreme view holds that the Bible is such a difficult and complex book that only professional Scripture scholars can fully understand it. Without knowledge of Hebrew and Greek, an advanced degree in Scripture, and a major commitment of time to study Scripture, no one can hope to surmount the complexities of Scripture and fully understand it, according to this view.

The error in this approach is obvious. It reduces the word of God to an object for scholarly study, and limits its readers to professional scholars. However valuable professional biblical scholarship is, God's revelation is addressed to more than professional Scripture scholars; it is addressed to every one of us.

On the other extreme is the view that God will speak so simply and directly to the hearts of every reader through Scripture that no problems of understanding will arise. This view holds that since the Bible is the word of God, it must be a word uttered in such a straightforward way that even the simplest person can immediately understand it.

This view has obvious appeal. It recognizes that God's word is addressed to all people, and addressed to them in an understandable manner. However, it misunderstands how God does speak to human beings. Quite often—and quite tragically—adherents of this view fail to hear God properly. In practice, the idea that God speaks simply to the reader of Scripture can mean that Scripture means what it means to *me*—the individual reader. An "objective" meaning of Scripture becomes elusive. The fact that many sects and denominations who profess to believe "only and all" that Scripture teaches also significantly disagree on just what Scripture does teach should alert us that the matter is not so simple.

The truth lies between these two views.

The Bible does contain God's word to us. But listening to it and understanding it requires study as well as an open heart. The lesson that we can learn from the Ethiopian is that good will is not enough in itself. God does not speak to us so simply through Scripture that we can expect to immediately and correctly understand every passage that we read. We must be willing to make an effort to understand the message of Scripture.

Our study of Scripture, and study about Scripture, is both necessary and wise. God does not call all of us to become Scripture scholars, but he does expect us to use the means available to better understand his word to us. Understanding his word requires more than an open heart (although it certainly requires that); understanding his word also requires a willing mind, an eager mind.

Our study of the Bible is an effort on our part to take Scripture seriously. We take it seriously when we are willing to let our lives be remade by what it says; we also take it seriously when we are concerned to find out just what it does say. If we are content to take the first meaning that pops into our head as the "meaning" of Scripture, we not only risk arriving at some very mistaken interpretations; we also show a disregard for Scripture itself. If Scripture has been inspired by God for our reading and instruction, we must respect it enough to be willing to study it.

The Holy Spirit's inspiration is not given to us so that we can forego the normal "human" means to help us understand Scripture. The inspiration of the Holy Spirit is enhanced, not inhibited, by proper study and diligent effort on our part. He does not wish to impart wisdom to us despite our willful ignorance.

We will be confronted with our ignorance as we read the Bible. We may become lost in the obscurity of some books or passages. Questions may come to our minds. They may be simple questions: "How did Jonah breathe in the belly of the fish?" They may be questions of fact: "Why are there often two different accounts of the same event recorded in the Bible—and which of them is right?" They may be questions of belief: "Do I have to believe that the world will end in the manner described in the Book of Revelation?" They may be questions regarding one's own life: "Should I give away my possessions and become a pacifist, as the words of Jesus seem to urge?"

Sometimes the significance of even the plainest passages escapes us. In this, we may have as many questions as Jesus' first followers, the apostles, had: "Then taking the Twelve aside he said to them, 'Now we are going up to Jerusalem, and everything that is written by the prophets about the Son of Man is to come true. For he will be handed over to the pagans and will be mocked, maltreated and spat on, and when they have scourged him they will put him to death; and on the third day he will rise again.' But they could make nothing of this; what he said was quite obscure to them, they had no idea what it meant" (Lk 18:31-34 JB).

Jesus' words were plain enough, but the apostles did not understand them. Luke emphasizes their bewilderment with a threefold repetition, a device often used in Scripture to stress a point: "But they could make nothing of this; what he said was quite obscure to them, they had no idea what it meant." It is significant that Jesus was not merely trying to teach the apostles, but was trying to explain the significance of Old Testament prophecies. The apostles basically failed to understand the Old Testament.

The apostles were not condemned to remain in ignorance forever. After Jesus' resurrection, he did explain again how he had fulfilled the prophecies of the Old Testament, and gave them the enlightenment to understand his explanation: "And he said to them, 'This is what I meant by saying, while I was still with you, that everything written about me in the Law of Moses and in the prophets and psalms was bound to be fulfilled.' Then he opened their minds to understand the Scriptures" (Lk 24:44-45 NEB).

Jesus still stands by our sides today to do for us what he did for the apostles: to make plain the meaning of the Scriptures for us and to open our minds to understand them. He does this through his Holy Spirit, whom we can rely upon to guide our study and bring the words of Scripture to life.

Some of the questions that come to our minds as we read the Bible may not admit of easy answers. But the better we understand Scripture, and the better we understand how God wishes to communicate to us through the words of Scripture, the more easily our questions will be resolved. As we grow in our understanding of the type of book the Bible is, we may find that we have been asking the wrong questions. Our study of Scripture and about Scripture can help resolve this difficulty.

However, we should always keep the goal of study in mind.

We make the effort to study the Bible (and not merely read it) so we can listen more clearly to the word of God speaking to us through the words of Scripture. Our study is not for its own sake. We do not study so that we can become experts in the Bible just as some are experts in the history of the American Civil War. Our study is for the sake of our prayerful use of Scripture, so that we may encounter the Word of God there, and find life in that word.

SOME PRINCIPLES OF STUDY

Our task in reading any book is to understand what its author intended to convey. The first and most important principle of Scripture study is exactly the same: to understand Scripture is to understand what its divine and human authors intended to convey by the words they used, the form they chose, and the ideas they expressed. To understand God speaking through Scripture we must understand the words of Scripture as they were written under the inspiration of God.

A passage of Scripture means what the authors intended it to mean when they wrote it. There can be, to be sure, extended meanings and interpretations given to passages, meanings which go beyond what the authors had in mind when they wrote. However helpful and exciting such interpretations may be, they are not the basic meaning of the passage. The basic meaning is that intended by the author. All additional or extended interpretations must be based upon this fundamental meaning and be extensions of it. Extended interpretations are not valid if they are opposed to the basic meaning intended by the author, or if they are held in place of it.

For example, Paul intended to convey something to the Corinthians when he wrote his letters to them. Because Paul wrote under the inspiration of the Holy Spirit, what he intended to convey and what God intended to convey were the same. God did not use Paul to teach something that Paul himself did not understand, or something he was not aware that he was saying. If the *real* meanings contained in the letters to the Corinthians were something that Paul himself was not aware of when he was writing, God would in effect have been using Paul as an unthinking dictating machine. Rather, the meaning inspired by God was a meaning that Paul himself grasped and intended to write. Paul himself insisted that "there are no hidden meanings in our letters besides what you can read for yourselves and understand" (2 Cor 1:13 JB).

Thus, Paul should be able to understand and agree with the interpretation we give to his letters to Corinth. What is inspired in Scripture is the basic meaning that the author understood and intended to convey to the reader.

The Church has stressed this point repeatedly. For example, St. Augustine insisted that the sense intended by the author was the sense inspired by the Holy Spirit, and hence the sense to be read as the Word of God. In his book *On Christian Doctrine,* he wrote that in order "to understand the divine oracles properly, there must be a constant effort to reach the mind of the author. It is through him that the Holy Spirit has spoken." Therefore, "it is a mistake to give Scripture a meaning different from the one intended by the writers, even when such an interpretation serves to foster charity and so stays in the realm of truth."

This does not mean that we cannot apply the Bible to our lives today. We can, we must, and we will. However, we must apply Scripture to our lives within the framework of the meaning its authors intended it to have at the time and place in which they wrote. Sometimes their meaning will be clear and its application to our lives will be immediate. Other times, it will not be so clear, and we will have to work hard to grasp the meaning the authors of Scripture intended their words to have. We must do this, because their meaning is God's meaning. No other meaning can replace it.

An important step in grasping the basic meaning intended by the authors is to understand the sense in which they used the words they wrote. When Old Testament writers referred to God as the "lion of Judah," they did not intend to picture God as an actual lion, comparable to the animals worshipped by some of the neighbors of the Israelites. They intended their words to be understood in a figurative, not a literal sense; they intended to convey an impression of the power of God.

We understand that when Christ said, "There was a man going down from Jerusalem to Jericho who fell prey to robbers. ..." (Lk 10:30 NAB), he was teaching by means of a parable—a fictional incident. To ask whether the incident *really* happened or not is to miss the point and to misunderstand what Christ intended to teach. The meaning of the parable is not that there once actually *was* a man on his way down from Jerusalem to Jericho who was robbed. The message Christ intended to teach had to do with love of our neighbor; he was not giving the latest Jericho road crime report.

The Book of Jonah may also be considered a parable. Its historical roots are weak: there is no trace in other biblical documents, or in Assyrian documents of the time, of any conversion of Nineveh and its king to the God of Israel. Excavations have revealed that Nineveh was a city of no more than three square miles, not "an exceedingly great city, three days' journey in breadth" (Jon 3:3 RSV). Even leaving the matter of the fish aside, it seems clear that the author of Jonah was not trying to write history.

The author of Jonah did intend to teach something about mercy and willingness to forgive. He intended to correct the narrow nationalism of the Jews after their return from exile, and to show that God's love extended even to non-Jews. He was not trying to teach about the stomach capacity of fish any more than Jesus was trying to teach about the crime rate on the Jericho road. To ask whether Jonah was *really* swallowed by a fish is similar to asking whether a man was *really* robbed on the Jericho road. Such a question entirely misses the point the author intended to make, and hence misunderstands the message inspired by God.

It is therefore important that in our reading of Scripture we understand whether the authors intended their words to have a literal or a figurative meaning. Words always have a literal meaning—but that is sometimes not the meaning inspired by God.

We must therefore make an effort to understand the different literary forms, the different types of writing, used by the authors of Scripture. Different books of the Bible were written in different ways for different purposes. The Bible contains books of history, books of prayer, books of advice, books of rules, books setting down the good news of what God did in Jesus Christ. Sometimes the same book will contain different kinds of writings, and sometimes will apparently have been written by more than one human author.

We must realize that the Bible is not a seamless garment. It is a quilt cut of many different kinds of cloth, woven in different stitches, and sewn together over a period of centuries. The design of the quilt is God's, to be sure, but the weavers and the cutters and the sewers were human. We cannot hop from one part of the quilt to another and expect to find the same fabric in the same color in the same weave.

In other words, the Bible is a library of books. It is not the single "book" that it appears to be when we pick it up, one integrated volume like a thick novel or textbook. The word "Bible" means "book." And for Christians the Bible is indeed "the book" because it contains the revelation of God. No other book can rank with it. But within the Bible we shall find many books written in different literary forms.

Some of the books of the Bible were written as a kind of history. Kings and Chronicles fall into this category. But they are not written as a modern historian would write history: the Hebrew historian was much more interested in the significance of events than in accurately recording the details of what happened. Hence different accounts of the same event may differ in their details, but will generally agree in the significance to be attributed to the event.

Some parts of the Bible, like the first eleven chapters of Genesis, may look like history but are really something different. The authors and editors of Genesis wished to teach about the condition of the human race and its relationship to God. They did not intend to teach, and were not inspired to teach, about geological processes of creation.

Not even all of Paul's epistles are cut from the same mold. His letter to Philemon is a genuine letter, written from one person to another, much as we would write a letter today. However,

Paul's letter to Rome more resembles a doctrinal essay than a purely personal letter.

The forms of writing in the Bible are as varied as the forms of writing in a popular magazine. When we read a magazine, we know that it will contain some articles which intend to present facts and information. It may also contain short stories, whose purpose is not to present factual information but to provide entertainment or insight. It may contain poetry, with dazzling visual imagery. It may contain an editorial, whose purpose will not be to present objective information in a detached manner but to convince us of a point of view. It will also contain ads, designed to get us to buy something.

If we confuse these different types of writing, the magazine will leave us in a muddle. But we don't: we know that the exaggerated claims of ads must be taken with a grain of salt. We apply very different criteria to factual articles, opinionated editorials, fictional short stories, and lyrical poetry.

We sometimes read the Bible with considerably less intelligence than we read popular magazines. We lump together vastly different kinds of writing as if they were all the same, written by a single hand at a single sitting. But God in his generosity has given us an entire library in the Bible—a library written over a period of a thousand years, by many hands in many different literary forms. Yet God's generosity also makes demands on us— the readers of the library. We must take care to understand the meaning of the many authors and the many forms they used.

Unless we have some basic appreciation for the kind of biblical book we are reading and the inspired intent of the author in writing it, our understanding of Scripture will remain superficial. Our ability to listen to God speak to us through the words of Scripture will be hampered. We may confuse his voice with our own muddled interpretations.

PRACTICAL APPROACHES TO STUDY

Study is merely sustained, serious reading: reading to understand. The distinctions between light reading and serious reading, and between serious reading and study, are often vague. Study is not something ominous or magical; it is simply careful reading—reading for meaning, reading using such aids as commentaries or the footnotes in the edition of the Bible that we are using.

One way to begin our study is to approach a chapter or a book of the Bible in the same way we would go about studying a school textbook. We might read a passage or chapter through from beginning to end, getting the general meaning. Then we would go back and reread it slowly, sentence by sentence, paying particular attention to the meaning. We would make use of whatever study aids we have at our disposal.

Another approach might be to begin study of a book of Scripture by reading a brief introduction to it—either in the edition of the Bible that we are using or in a book which discusses the books of Scripture. Then we might read the book of Scripture itself, as a whole, consulting the footnotes to see if they offer any enlightenment. After going through the book once, we would go back and reread the passages that strike us as the most significant. If we are studying a Gospel, we might check the other Gospels to see how the other evangelists presented the same incident. Naturally, except for very short books, this will probably not all be done at one sitting.

Many people find it very helpful to mark certain verses or passages as they read, underlining important words or highlighting certain sections by drawing a line alongside them in the margin. This can be a very good and useful practice, and help us both understand and remember what we read.

We should not be afraid to mark up our Bible as we read. There is nothing irreverent about this: the word of God is best honored by the place we give it in our minds and hearts, not the place we give it on a living room table. Our Bibles are meant for our use and understanding. We should mark with some caution, however; the passage we heavily underline with ballpoint pen today might not be the passage that speaks meaningfully to us tomorrow. It is better to use pencil and mark lightly, leaving room to mark something else the next time we read the same passage.

As we read for understanding, the question that should be foremost in our minds is, "What is the point that the authors are trying to make? What are they trying to convey?" This is the question that is unconsciously in our minds when we read most things: an editorial in the evening newspaper, instructions for assembling a tricycle, a magazine article on heart disease. Our first approach to understanding the Bible should be the same: we read in order to grasp what is said. If we are overawed by the holiness of God's word, and strain too hard to hear what God is saying to us, we may miss the obvious meaning that the words themselves convey. Yet the words themselves must be the starting point in our understanding Scripture and listening to God speak to us through it. In one sense, we must read the Bible as we would read any other book in order to truly understand that the Bible is unlike any other book. We must ask, "What are the authors saying?" "What are they trying to convey?" "What is the point they are making?"

As with any book, we must pay attention to the particular context in which individual verses and passages occur. Quoting out of context distorts or destroys the meaning.

We must also be alert to the broad context of the entire Bible. Each book finds its setting and meaning within the work of God which began in Abraham and culminated in the early Church. The Bible is an expression of that work of God, and each book in it captures some segment or aspect of it. Each book then finds its ultimate meaning not in itself, but in the context of the entire Bible. As we read a passage or book we should be alert to the light that other passages and books throw upon the one that we are reading. We must be alert to the place that a book occupies in the sweep of salvation history. We need to ask, "Why was this book written? Who was it written for?"

As we read, we should put ourselves "at the scene" of what we are reading. If we are reading a passage from the Gospels, we should note not only what Jesus taught, but to whom he taught it and what their reaction was. We might imagine what our reaction would have been had we been on the scene ourselves. Quite often those who first listened to Jesus were astonished by sayings we read quite calmly today: "After hearing it, many of his followers said, 'This is intolerable language. How could anyone accept it?'" (Jn 6:60 JB). Perhaps we are missing an important dimension and should be astonished too. Do we too easily pass over hard sayings of Jesus as if they were not hard sayings?

If we are reading from one of the Old Testament prophets, we must keep in mind the state of the chosen people at the time the prophet was speaking. The prophets spoke to specific situations at different moments of history. Was the observance of the Law in a time of decay, and was destruction of the nation looming, or was the prophet rather speaking a word of comfort to a people already dispersed in exile?

We also need to learn from the Bible about the life and culture of ancient Israel and bring that knowledge to our further reading. Many of the biblical references to water and streams take on their fullest meaning when we realize that the Israelites spent their earliest years wandering as nomads in the desert, living from water hole to water hole. The familiar verse about not lighting a lamp and putting it under a bushel, but upon a stand where it can give light to all in the house, becomes most vivid when we realize that many families lived in one-room houses.

We do not have to make a study of ancient life and culture as much as be attentive to the clues contained in Scripture and slowly absorb a feeling for what life was like then. Our aim is not to become experts about ancient times, but to appreciate the meaning that the words of Scripture had for its first listeners. In order to listen to the word of God speak to us in the twentieth century, we must strive to listen to the prophets as sixth-century B.C. inhabitants of Jerusalem did; we must sit at the feet of Jesus as first-century disciples. If we rush by this first step, we will miss much of what Scripture can teach us.

In summary, the goal of our study is to determine the meaning that the authors had in mind when they wrote. We will want to understand the words they used in the sense they intended to use them. We will want to understand each verse in terms of its context, following the authors' line of thought as they present their material.

Study about Scripture should never replace reading of Scripture, and reading of Scripture should never replace prayerful meditation on Scripture and its application to daily life. A balance is necessary. It is essential to be faithful to a daily prayerful reflection on a passage from Scripture. To regularly study a book of Scripture, or a major portion of a book of Scripture, with the help of a good introduction and notes (and perhaps a commentary) provides the background for selective meditative reading. To study a book about Scripture occasionally is almost essential, if our understanding of Scripture is to mature and grow. But neither type of study should replace our basic daily fifteen-minute Scripture reading; both will require time of their own.

Scripture is a book of life; it is also a book which a lifetime cannot exhaust. Our study of it should be steady—neither overwhelmed by the amount we have yet to learn, nor lazy in making the sustained effort required.

USING STUDY AIDS

There are many sources available for our study of Scripture, many more than we probably realize.

The first source for our study should be the Bible itself. The Bible explains itself—in the sense that a familiarity with the whole of Scripture will make the individual books and passages easier to understand. As we grow in our understanding of the Old Testament, our understanding of the New Testament will take on greater depth. As we become acquainted with all of Paul's epistles, and with his missionary activities described in the Acts of the Apostles, his individual epistles will become easier to understand. As we learn more about the customs and culture of first-century Palestine, the words and actions of Jesus will become more significant for us.

Because the Bible illuminates and explains itself, we will need to grow in our familiarity with the Bible and our ability to find our way through it. Many editions of the Bible include cross references to other portions of the Bible that are similar to the passage being read. Sometimes these Scripture references are listed in the margin; sometimes they are indicated in notes at the bottom of the page. Different editions and translations of the Bible handle them differently, and many editions do not include any. However, if the Bible you read does have them and if you know how to make use of them, they can add a new depth of meaning to your understanding of Scripture and provide a simple means of Scripture study.

Sometimes cross references indicate where else in Scripture a passage can be found that is virtually identical to the passage we are reading. These types of references are particularly frequent for the Gospels of Matthew, Mark, and Luke, since many incidents and teachings from the life of Jesus are included in two or three of these Gospels. Since different Gospel writers often present the same incident with slightly different emphases, by comparing two or three accounts we can notice details we would otherwise overlook. It is by comparing accounts of Peter's denials in Matthew and Luke, for example, that we notice that it was his accent which identified him as a Galilean.

Often cross references in the New Testament point to the location of a passage in the Old Testament that is being quoted by Jesus or a New Testament writer. Looking up the Old Testament passage and reading it in its original context can often help us better understand the point that Jesus or Paul is making.

Sometimes cross references indicate where we can find another passage that is concerned with the same issue or makes a similar point—or, sometimes, presents an opposing view. For example, comparing the apparent contradiction between Luke 12:37 and Luke 17:7-8 prepares us for the teaching of Jesus in Luke 22:27, but we might miss this without cross references that direct our attention to the relationship between these passages.

Another convenient source for our study can be the footnotes provided in the various editions of the Bible. Footnotes can range in context and quality from entirely useless to highly useful. Among the more useful footnotes are those which offer some clarification of obscure passages, and which trace the development of the theme of the passage. If this type of footnote provides cross references, simply looking up the other passages referred to and reading them in context can provide food for study.

Practically speaking it can sometimes be helpful to glance at the footnotes for a chapter before beginning to read the chapter. Sometimes it takes only a few seconds to discover that the notes for a particular chapter aren't very helpful, and can be ignored in our reading. Sometimes one or two of the notes will stand out as worth study; if we already have a general familiarity with the particular Scripture reading we are doing that day, we might want to study these notes right away, so that our later reading of the words of Scripture can be uninterrupted.

Many editions of the Bible contain maps, and they can also be useful in our study. Perhaps the most subtle way that we can undermine the power of Scripture and fail to read it as God's word to us is to treat it as a collection of writings from some other world, a holy world that has no connection with the one we live in. We will not consciously read the Bible as a book describing make-believe people living in a make-believe land, but we can unconsciously come pretty close to doing so. We can treat the people of the Bible as if they are entirely unlike you and me, and we can view the world they live in as being completely different from ours.

One modest way of bridging the gap between the world of Scripture and our world is to make a special effort to transpose the geographic world of the Bible into the modern world by matching up the cities and countries of the Bible with modern cities and countries. Jerusalem is Jerusalem and Rome is Rome, of course. But do we consciously realize when we read of Paul's journeys that he was traveling mostly through the modern countries of Turkey and Greece? Do we locate Old Testament events which took place in Babylon and Persia as occurring in the modern countries of Iraq and Iran?

Making such a transposition as we read takes only a few minutes with the help of a good biblical map such as is contained in many Bibles. But even this simple step can help remind us that the word of God was spoken in our world, that Jesus Christ walked among us, that what we read in Scripture is a word addressed to our world and to us.

To continue to grow in our understanding of the individual books of Scripture, more comprehensive study aids are necessary. It is helpful to have something available which discusses the type of literature a given book of Scripture is, the background of its composition (to the extent that this is known) and the main themes that are discussed in it. Making use of such a study aid before reading (or rereading) a book of the Bible can lay the groundwork for greater understanding by preparing us for what we will find there.

It is perhaps unnecessary to repeat that such study aids about the Bible should never replace reading of Scripture itself. But neither can such study aids be dispensed with as unhelpful. If one were to take a summer trip with his or her family, visiting the historic sites of the American Civil War, it would be helpful to consult a map beforehand, and study a tour guide with brief explanations of the major battle sites. Reading a map can never replace making the actual trip, but it can help one find where he or she is going. What may only appear to be a grassy meadow might, with the help of a tour guide, be appreciated as having historical significance as a battlefield—although merely reading about it in the tour guide is lifeless compared with actually visiting it.

So too with Scripture. Having some idea of the nature of a book of Scripture can help us avoid getting lost in it. Knowing something about the authors' concerns can help us understand better the significance of what they wrote. But our maps and tour guides to Scripture cannot replace our actual reading and study of Scripture itself.

The most convenient overall study aids will be the introductions to the individual books of Scripture provided in many editions of the Bible. These will vary in quality and scope, but can give the reader some orientation to what he or she is about to read. They should not be overlooked, or left unread.

In particular, a good introduction can go a long way in making a book of the Old Testament intelligible—if only by providing the setting in which the book was written. To return to the analogy of the Bible as a quilt: it is often enlightening to know when a particular square of cloth was woven, and by whom, and in what setting. The theology of the Jews in exile has its differences from the theology of the Jews reigning gloriously under David. The literary form of the Book of Daniel has important differences from the literary form of Deuteronomy. Adequate introductions can alert us to the unique character of each book, and help us avoid falling into a "Bible as seamless garment" mentality.

The *Oxford Annotated Bible with the Apocrypha* editions of the *Revised Standard Version* has excellent notes and introductions and is now available in the *New Revised Standard Version*. Excellent notes and introductions are found in the complete editions of the *New Jerusalem Bible;* its cheaper reader's editions contain very abbreviated notes, not nearly so helpful. Notes and introductions in the *New American Bible* are generally helpful, although not as complete as those in the *New Jerusalem Bible*.

Commentaries and books about Scripture must also have a place in our study. It is naïve to assume that twentieth-century Americans can intuitively grasp the cultural differences and nuances of the Israelite people of twenty-five hundred years ago, or even the political and religious culture of the first-century Judaism in which Jesus exercised his ministry. If the Bible contains the revelation of God in words of human beings, we must strive to understand those words as words of actual people. Like the Ethiopian, we must make a pilgrimage to Jerusalem. Like the Ethiopian, we must study writings that are "foreign" to us. The word of God came to the human race through specific individuals within a specific people—and finally through the specific person of Jesus Christ. Now for all time, all nations and all people must turn to these writings as the privileged source of God's revelation. Whatever the obstacles of language or culture, whatever the distance created by time and geography, we must enter into the world of Moses and Isaiah and Jesus to learn of God's intervention into human history. Books about Scripture can provide an indispensable help for us in doing this.

The vast number of commentaries, dictionaries, concordances, and books about the Bible prohibit any exhaustive listing, much less evaluation. I can mention a few that I have found personally useful, or which have been highly recommended to me.

A dictionary of the Bible will provide concise information about specific topics or themes or words. Several dictionaries provide a brief introduction to each book of the Bible. A dictionary of the Bible can be a handy and inexpensive reference work, to be consulted when we have a specific question to bring to it.

Detailed verse by verse (and even phrase by phrase) commentaries on the text of sacred Scripture are available. Most readers will make only occasional use of such commentaries, relying on them chiefly to check on the meaning of obscure verses. A more loosely constructed running commentary is probably more advisable for general usage, and can provide an invaluable help in making an in-depth study of one of the books of Scripture.

Perhaps the best bargain on the market, and the book to buy if your finances limit you to a very select number of reference works, is the *Dictionary of the Bible* by John McKenzie. Available in paperback, this general reference work of 800,000 words contains a wealth of reliable information.

Considerably more expensive is the *Jerome Bible Commentary*, edited by Brown, Fitzmyer, and Murphy. It is now available in a revised edition which is called the *New Jerome Bible Commentary*. In addition to containing a virtually line-by-line commentary on the entire Bible, the *Jerome* commentary contains introductory discussions of each book in the Bible, and more than twenty scholarly essays. It is not the kind of work the average reader will want to make constant reference to, but it can be a useful resource for answers to specific questions. It is the kind of book you will want to know where you can borrow when you need it, and perhaps hope to afford someday.

Much more reasonable in price are the series of commentaries published by the Liturgical Press of St. John's Abbey (Collegeville, Minnesota). *The Collegeville Bible Commentary—Old Testament Series* is published in 25 booklets; *The Collegeville Bible Commentary—New Testament Series* is published in 11 booklets. The advantage of this series is that one can purchase just those guides that are of specific interest: for most people, a commentary on the Gospel of John is more vital than a commentary on Leviticus. Most of the authors of the booklets in this series are well known and respected Scripture scholars. The individual pamphlets that I have made extensive use of have been very well done and very helpful. They are also published together in a two volume paperback (Old and New Testament) and one volume hardcover.

Concordances list, with varying degrees of completeness, the different places a given word is used in the Bible. A concordance is keyed to the occurrences of words (as opposed to ideas or themes), and hence each translation of Scripture must have its own concordance—since different translations will use different words in translating a Greek or Hebrew word. Further, since the same Greek word may be translated by different English words as the sense and context dictates, an English concordance is a tool of limited utility. Concordances which list the Greek or Hebrew words avoid this difficulty, but are difficult to use by someone not knowing Greek or Hebrew.

There are also many books giving an introduction to the Bible, or providing a study of a specific biblical theme. Browsing through a good religious bookstore (if one is nearby) is perhaps the best way to find those books that are suited to your needs and interests.

A final caution about study is necessary. Our study must not become a shield preventing us from hearing God's word; it must be a means of our hearing God's word with clarity. There must come a time in our daily reading when we shift our focus from trying to understand the Bible to trying to listen to the word of God speak to us through the words of Scripture. Our call is not to become Scripture scholars but disciples of Christ. Our study is a *preparatory* step; it must not become the final step in our reading. Study should give way to listening.

THREE

Listening

*That very same day, two of them were on their way to a village
called Emmaus, seven miles from Jerusalem, and they were talking together about all that had happened. Now as they talked
this over, Jesus himself came up and walked by their side; but
something prevented them from recognizing him.*

*He said to them, "You foolish men! So slow to believe the full
message of the prophets! Was it not ordained that the Christ
should suffer and so enter into his glory?" Then, starting with
Moses and going through all the prophets, he explained to them
the passages throughout the Scriptures that were about himself.*

*While he was with them at table, he took the bread and said
the blessing; then he broke it and handed it to them. And their
eyes were opened and they recognized him; but he had vanished
from their sight. Then they said to each other, "Did not our
hearts burn within us as he talked to us on the road and explained the Scriptures to us?"* Luke 24:13-16, 25-27, 30-32 JB

W E CAN ASSUME that the followers of Jesus were well
acquainted with their Scriptures—the books that we read
as the Old Testament. They had studied these books and made a
serious effort to understand God's word and God's laws. Yet
despite this study, and despite their association with Jesus Christ,
they failed to see that he had fulfilled the Scriptures.

Jesus used their knowledge of the Scriptures as the basis for
explaining his own mission. He explained the significance of the

Scriptures, throwing new light on familiar passages, showing the connection between what the prophets foretold and his own life. Through Jesus' explanation, the two disciples not only came to a new understanding of the Old Testament; they came to a deeper understanding of Jesus himself.

The words of Jesus not only gave them enlightenment and knowledge; his words also touched their hearts. "Did not our hearts burn within us as he talked to us on the road and explained the Scriptures to us?" The words of Jesus to them were not abstract words, words without connection to their lives. They were words of life, words which sank into their very beings and changed their lives.

Jesus frequently explained the meaning of the Scriptures to his followers. In Luke's Gospel, Jesus' first sermon in Nazareth is an explanation of a passage from the prophet Isaiah. Jesus made the bold claim, "This text is being fulfilled today even as you listen" (Lk 4:21 JB). He often had to explain his parables to his followers: "His disciples asked him what this parable might mean, and he said, 'The mysteries of the kingdom of God are revealed to you; for the rest there are only parables, so that they may see but not perceive, listen but not understand'" (Lk 8:9-10 JB). And the instructions he gave his followers just before he ascended into heaven began with a final explanation of the significance of the Old Testament: "'This is what I meant when I said, while I was still with you, that everything written about me in the Law of Moses, in the Prophets and in the Psalms, has to be fulfilled.' He then opened their minds to understand the Scripture" (Lk 24:44-45 JB).

On all these occasions, Jesus' words brought more than new understanding to the disciples. They were words of life, words that touched the disciples' hearts and changed their lives. When Jesus spoke, something happened. When he said to a sick man, "Be healed!" the man was healed. When he invited someone to "Follow me," the person's life was changed. When he spoke to the apostles about the Father's love and care for them, we must imagine that their hearts burned within them as they listened.

Our hearts too would burn within us if Jesus would walk by

our side, explaining the meaning of Scripture to us. We can read his words in the New Testament, but sometimes they seem lifeless—perhaps too familiar and shopworn, perhaps too obscure. Sometimes too we listen but do not perceive, read but do not understand. We wish we could read the words of the Old Testament in such a way that Jesus would shine through them, so that we could share the understanding that the two disciples received as they walked the road to Emmaus with Jesus.

But Jesus *is* there by our side—just as he walked beside the disciples on the road to Emmaus. He will explain the Scriptures to us and touch our hearts as we learn to listen to him in our reading. We therefore need to go about reading Scripture in such a way that he can speak to our hearts as well as our minds. We need to learn how to listen; we need the inspiration of the Holy Spirit in our listening.

ATTITUDES

To hear the Lord's voice as the disciples did, we must approach Scripture with the right attitudes of mind and heart. To hear the word of God in Scripture, we must read Scripture as being truly the word of God—with all the reverence and awe that suggests. We must approach Scripture with an open heart, with eagerness to obey the word when we hear it, and with faith that we will hear God's word for us personally.

Reading Scripture this way requires us to get our study into perspective. We need to study the books of the Bible much as we would study any other set of books—in order to gain an understanding of them. Much of our study will be (and rightfully should be) *about* the Bible. But this must never be an end in itself; rather, it should be a step preparing us to read the Bible with understanding so that we can listen to the voice of God speak to us through its words. We need to go beyond studying the Bible and simply *read* it as the word of God.

When we drive a car, we are usually not aware of the windshield. We look through the windshield in order to see where we are going; we do not look *at* the windshield and make it the focus of our attention. A dirty windshield can obscure our vision and distract us. Then we need to stop the car and clean the windshield. And to do a good job, we will have to look at the windshield instead of through it.

Our study of the Bible is like cleaning the windshield. We need to look *at* the Bible in order to study it and grow in our understanding of it. We need to learn how the Bible came to be written; we need to learn about each book of the Bible; we need to compare translations to see how each one interprets difficult verses. But none of this is really reading Scripture as the word of God, anymore than looking at the windshield of a car is the same as looking through it. Study can even distract us from hearing God's word, just as staring at the bug spots on a windshield may cause us to drive off the road. We must get beyond our study of the Bible if the Scriptures are to be a vehicle for us to hear the word of God. The Bible must become for us a window to God.

The epistle of James uses a similar analogy in teaching us how to listen correctly to the word of God: "Accept and submit to the word which has been planted in you and can save your souls. But you must do what the word tells you, and not just listen to it and deceive yourselves. To listen to the word and not obey is like looking at your own features in a mirror and then, after a quick look, going off and immediately forgetting what you looked like" (Jas 1:21-24 JB). Scripture can be a mirror in which we see and understand ourselves. It can give us a glimpse of ourselves through the eyes of God. But we must look at ourselves in the mirror, and not at the mirror itself.

James' main point in this passage is that we must obey the word of God: "But those who look into the perfect law, the law of liberty, and persevere, being not hearers who forget but doers who act—they will be blessed in their doing" (Jas 1:25 NRSV). Scripture is unlike any other book in that it makes a claim on our lives. If we read the Bible with the detachment we usually bring to a book, we will not be reading it as the word of God. We cannot remain aloof if we wish God to speak to us.

The fundamental attitude that we must bring to Scripture is an open heart: an eagerness to listen to the word of God and a willingness to heed it. If we want God to speak to us but are not interested in really listening to him, we do him a discourtesy, just as we would be discourteous if we were to ask someone a question and then walk away in the middle of his or her answer. To want God to speak to us, but reserve our judgment on whether to take his words seriously or not, is to treat his voice as merely one opinion among many, and not as the voice of God.

The teaching of Jesus is clear: "Whoever has my commandments and observes them is the one who loves me" (Jn 14:21 NAB). "It is not those who say to me, 'Lord, Lord,' who will enter the kingdom of heaven, but the person who does the will of my Father in heaven.... Therefore everyone who *listens* to these words of mine *and acts on them* will be like a sensible man who built his house on rock" (Mt 7:21, 24 JB).

An attitude of obedience is necessary if we are to read Scripture as the word of God. We are not the judges of God's word; his word is our judge. To place limits on what we will allow God to ask of us is to refuse to listen to him. A difference of opinion with God is sin; failure to carry out his commands is disobedience. Our obedience is not to laws and codes, but to the God who created us. It is not an obedience of mere external observance, but the entrusting of our whole selves to God.

Our attitude in approaching Scripture must recognize that God wishes to speak to each of us personally. The Bible is not a book that merely reveals something about God and his presence in history. If we read it as the word of God, it is also a personal communication to each of us. The Holy Spirit is present in us, inspiring us when we read Scripture. When we read it, the word of God can speak to each of us as individuals.

When we check our mail box each day, we find different kinds of mail in it. We receive ads addressed "Dear Occupant." We receive bills which have our name on them, but which were sent to us by a computer. They are a more personal kind of mail than the "Dear Occupant" letters, but we know that the computer is less interested in our names than in our account numbers. We might also receive a mimeographed letter from an acquaintance who has gone overseas, and who wants to write back to a number of friends to tell them news. This is more personal than a computerized bill even though it was sent to a number of people besides ourselves. And finally, we might receive a letter from our father. This we would open first and read eagerly. It would be written and addressed to us in a truly personal way. It would be a greeting from someone who knows us very well and loves us very much.

If we read Scripture as the word of God, we must read it as a letter that comes from our Father to us as individuals. The Bible is not addressed to "Dear Occupant" as an ad for heaven sent to the human race. It is not impersonally addressed to us, like the bills and overdue notices sent by a computer. And even though the Scriptures are for all men and women, God's voice does not address us all alike, as a mimeographed newsletter does. God's voice speaks to each of us individually, as a father writes to each of his children. If we approach Scripture correctly, we will read it as a Father's message sent to each of us by name.

Comparing Scripture to a personal letter also gives us a clue to its deepest meaning. When a close friend or relative writes to us, they often tell us what is going on in their lives—perhaps the birth of a new child, perhaps moving to a new home, perhaps just simple events of daily life. Our friends and relatives do not wish to convey mere information about themselves, as if we needed more facts to fill out a biography. The reason our friends write is to reveal themselves to us, because they love us and we love them. They send a letter not to transmit a set of facts, but to express themselves personally. Both the sending and the receiving of the letter have meaning because of the bond of love that exists between us and them. The letter is an expression of that love, and a means of allowing that love to grow.

So too with Scripture. God does not want to reveal facts so much as to reveal himself. He does not write to us because we are compiling his biography, but because he loves us and invites us to love him. Scripture is an expression of God himself and an expression of love for us. It is one of his means of personally inviting us to enter into a relationship of love with him. If we miss this basic focus, we miss the meaning of Scripture—no matter how well we might otherwise understand the facts and truths contained in Scripture.

It is easy for us today to be merely spectators of life. We can watch films of floods and wars on the evening news—and get up to get a snack during the commercial. We are able to see reports of terrifying events without having to get personally involved. This mere-observer attitude can unconsciously carry over into our reading of Scripture: we can read its words as true and important—but as not affecting us.

Personal involvement is different from detached observation. If we were driving along a deserted highway and were the first to arrive at the scene of a serious car accident, we would be thrust into that situation. We would be faced with decisions: do we move the injured from their cars because of danger of fire, or would that aggravate their injuries? How do we stop serious bleeding? What should we do when someone is literally dying before our eyes? Our hearts would pound, our minds work feverously to think of the right thing to do. How different it is to be there than to see a report of the accident on television!

Our encounter with the word of God in Scripture should be real and immediate to us. Not that our hearts should pound every time we read the Bible, but there should be a sense of immediacy about what we read. The Bible is not simply a report of the word of God spoken long ago, like a magazine article. It is the word of God being spoken to us here and now as we read. We cannot be detached observers; we must hear it as personally addressed to us, inviting and demanding our personal response.

If we bring to Scripture an attitude that it is God's word to us, we will experience it as that. If we come before God eager to listen to what he would say to us, we will find that he does speak to us. His word in Scripture will come alive for us. We will read it not as a dead letter written long ago but as a word spoken to us today, a word of life in Jesus Christ.

APPROACHES

We must therefore approach Scripture in prayer. I have mentioned earlier how important it is to begin our daily reading time with the prayer that God will speak to us through the words of Scripture; I can only emphasize this once more. We need to faithfully pray that the Lord will speak to us through our reading of his word. We need to believe that he hears our prayer and will answer it.

Prayer places us consciously in the presence of God. To listen to him speak through the words of Scripture, we need to be alone with him and his word. We need to be as free from distractions as possible, concentrating only on him and what he would say to us. If we are going to listen to his voice, we need to still all other voices, especially our mental wanderings. We do not need to strain to be alone with God's word; we need rather to relax with it, and simply focus on him who is speaking to us. This too is the concern of our beginning prayer, to help us become alone with God. The Lord invites us to "be still and know that I am God" (Ps 46:10 RSV).

As we begin our reading of Scripture, we should take the approach that "What I am reading is written to me. What I am reading is written about me." If we are reading the words of Jesus, we should read them as personally addressed to us. If we read a letter from Paul, we should read it as a letter written to us—as if it had been delivered in that morning's mail.

To read and apply Scripture so personally may seem like an unwarranted liberty. But St. Paul uses Scripture this way in his epistles. He draws from incidents in the Old Testament and applies them to the lives of those to whom he writes.

Paul wrote to the Corinthians, "I want to remind you, brothers, how our fathers were all guided by a cloud above them and how they all passed through the sea.... In spite of this, most of them failed to please God and their corpses littered the desert. These things all happened as warnings for us, not to have the wicked lusts for forbidden things that they had.... All of this happened to them as a warning, and it was written down to be a lesson for all of us who are living at the end of the age" (1 Cor 10:1, 5-6, 11). The word translated here as "warning" could also be translated "example" or "type": the events of the Old Covenant were types anticipating the fulfillment of the New Covenant. Similarly the events of both the Old and New Testaments are examples for us, instructing us in how the plan of God is being fulfilled in our lives today.

Paul also quotes from the Old Testament and makes direct application of its texts: "It is written in the Law of Moses: 'You shall not muzzle an ox while it treads out grain.' Is God concerned here for oxen, or does he not rather say this for our sakes? You can be sure it was *written* for *us*, for the plowman should plow in hope and the harvester expect a share in the grain. If we have sown for you in the spirit, is it too much to expect a material harvest from you?" (1 Cor 9:9-11 NAB). Again, in his letter to Rome, Paul discusses Abraham's faith and maintains that "Scripture however does not refer only to him but *to us* as well when it says that his faith was thus 'considered'; our faith too will be 'considered' if we believe in him who raised Jesus our Lord from the dead" (Rom 4:23-24 JB).

If we read Scripture in this way, we will understand both what the text meant when the author wrote it and what it means personally for us. When we hear the word of God addressed to Israel through the prophet Jeremiah, saying, "I have loved you with an everlasting love" (Jer 31:3 JB), we will understand these words to be God's assurance of his love for ancient Israel—their meaning when Jeremiah uttered them. But those words will also have a meaning for us today: we can listen to God speaking to us through those words, assuring us of his steadfast and everlasting love for us. We can read them in this way because that meaning is consistent with the meaning of the whole of Scripture and with our experience of God's love for us as members of the body of Christ. We can read Jeremiah's words as God's words addressed personally to us, giving us one more assurance of his love for us.

We can read Paul's letters in a similar way. Paul writes to the Ephesians, "May God give *you* the power through his Spirit for *your* hidden self to grow strong, so that Christ may live in *your* hearts through faith, and then, planted in love and built on love, *you* will with all the saints have strength to grasp the breadth and the length, the height and the depth; until, knowing the love of Christ, which is beyond all knowledge, *you* are filled with the utter fullness of God" (Eph 3:16-19 JB). The "you" Paul had in mind were people living in Ephesus almost two thousand years ago. But we can each read Paul's words today as God's words addressed to us by name. We can read them as revealing what God has in store for each one of us today.

"What I am reading is written to me. What I am reading is written about me." As we read Scripture in this way, the words will take on meaning and application for us.

When we hear Jesus say, "Remove the plank from your own eye before worrying about the splinter in your neighbor's eye," some of our neighbors and their splinters may come to mind—and some of our own planks as well. When we hear Jesus say, "Judge not, lest you be judged," some of our own unfounded condemnations of others may occur to us, as well as the areas of our lives where we hope for mercy and not strict judgment. Above all, when we hear him say, "I have come so that they may have life, and have it more abundantly," we will know that he is talking to us, saying that he came so that we may experience fullness of life. It is one thing for me to believe that Jesus came out of love for all men and women; it is another thing to accept that he loves *me*.

There are many of Jesus' sayings that must be read as words addressed personally to us if we are to truly understand them. He did not intend to merely leave behind him a body of general teachings, containing such principles as "He who loves his life will lose it"; "I am the resurrection and the life"; "Love one another." He intended that we hear his words as addressed specifically to us: "As I have loved *you*, so *you* must love one another." "I am the resurrection and the life for *you*."

Much of the Bible can easily be applied directly to our lives in this way; other parts, however, are more difficult to apply. What are we to make of some of the passages and incidents which seem to have little to say to us in a personal way?

Our approach must be to read some sections of Scripture as

being not so much spoken *to* us as *about* us. For example, the second book of Samuel tells how King David saw Bathsheba, the wife of Uriah the soldier, and desired her. David arranged for Uriah to be stationed at the front of the battle lines, where he was killed. The king then took Bathsheba as his own wife. This displeased God, who sent Nathan the prophet to David. Nathan told him:

> Judge this case for me! In a certain town there were two men, one rich, the other poor. The rich man had flocks and herds in great numbers. But the poor man had nothing at all except one little ewe lamb that he had bought. He nourished her, and she grew up with him and his children. She shared the little food he had and drank from his cup and slept in his bosom. She was like a daughter to him. Now the rich man received a visitor but he would not take from his own flocks and herds to prepare a meal for the wayfarer who had come to him. Instead he took the poor man's ewe lamb and made a meal of it for his visitor.   2 Samuel 12:1-4 NAB

David's anger flared up and he said: "As the Lord lives, the man who has done this merits death. He shall restore the ewe lamb fourfold because he has done this and has had no pity." And then Nathan said to David, "You are the man" (vv. 5-7 NAB).

We must say to ourselves as we read Scripture, "I am the man," or "I am the woman." The words of Scripture are talking about *me.*" It was not merely Peter who often misunderstood Jesus and acted without thinking; I often misunderstand and act rashly. It was not only the priest and Levite of the good Samaritan parable who pass by the injured man on Jericho road; I do the same, every day. It was not only Lazarus that Jesus loved and raised to life; he loves me, and wishes to raise me to life.

Reading Scripture in this personal way, as a word speaking to us and about us, does not of course excuse us from the responsibility of study. Unless we have made efforts to understand the meaning of the books and passages of the Bible, we may misunderstand them and misapply them to ourselves. If we fail to grasp the point of a parable, it won't do us any good to try to apply it to our lives.

For example, when Jesus warned the apostles that he was about to be put to death as a criminal and that a time of crisis was at hand, they took his injunction, "Let him who has no sword sell his mantle and buy one" (Lk 22:36 RSV), too literally. Their eager reply, "Look, Lord, here are two swords," drew a weary rebuke from Jesus: they had misunderstood his words again. It does us little good to eagerly respond to a word from Jesus if we misunderstand it. Therefore, our study of the Scriptures and their meaning is essential.

Yet it is also essential to bear in mind that the meaning of Scripture must become a meaning *for us*. We can have keen insight into the parable of the good Samaritan—but we will not be reading it as the word of God unless we understand how it applies to our own lives. "Which of these," Jesus asked, "proved himself a neighbor to the man who fell into the brigands' hands?" We can know the answer to that question quite easily. But the next verse brings the meaning home: "Go, and do the same yourself" (Lk 10:36-37 JB).

Even seemingly obscure sections of the Old Testament have their message for us. "Everything written before our time was written for our instruction, that we might derive hope from the lessons of patience and words of encouragement in the Scriptures" (Rom 15:4 NAB). It would be difficult to maintain that there is any section of Scripture that God cannot use to speak to us. We must make the effort to understand every part of Scripture that we read as teaching us something about ourselves in the sight of God, as conveying a message from God to us. We must be open to God speaking to us through even the most apparently unlikely passage, giving us an insight into its meaning.

GOD SPEAKS TO US

God will speak to those who prayerfully read the Bible as his word. He will not speak in an audible voice; he will not even form words in our mind. His speaking will use no other words than the words that we read—but those words will take on meaning and become alive as if God were present speaking them directly to us. We will have a strong sense that the words of Scripture are indeed addressed to us and are talking about us; we will have a sense that they have a meaning and application in our own lives and specific situations. The Bible will be not merely God's word, but God's word to me. Our hearts will burn within us as we read—not with violent emotion but with the gentle touch of the Holy Spirit, a peaceful presence within us, an assurance that the Father indeed loves us and calls us by name.

We cannot command God's speaking to us. We cannot stir up ourselves to make sure that something happens. Our part can only be to study, to pray, to read with an open and attentive heart, to listen. It is God's part to do the speaking, to give understanding to our minds and touch our hearts. We cannot control his graces. It is a mistake to try to "force" an experience of the Lord speaking to us. It is a mistake to demand that he speak more dramatically than he has chosen to. And it is above all a mistake to want to control what he has to say.

In all aspects of our spiritual lives there are times and seasons. Some days the words of Scripture will seem to leap off the page. Other days they will lie there, dead, uninspiring. For perhaps weeks at a time we will read with understanding and insight; at other stretches our reading may be so unrewarding that only our resolve to continue faithfully will keep us going. Sometimes the voice of the Lord will be one of comfort, consolation, care. At other times it will be a more severe voice, pointing out the price of discipleship, pointing out areas in our lives that must change, pointing out our sinfulness. The voice of the Lord is both gentle and severe, as we need to hear it.

The Lord will not limit his speaking to us through the words of Scripture to the times that we are actually reading Scripture. In my own life, I find that I often hear God speaking personally to me through Scripture when I listen to the texts of Scripture read during the celebration of the Liturgy. Perhaps this is as it should be; perhaps our hearing of the word of God should be literally a "hearing," and a hearing in the context of the Church gathered to listen to the word of God proclaimed to them. I do know that the reading and study of Scripture that I do outside the Liturgy has prepared me to listen to the word of God during the Liturgy. It was only after I had been faithful to a daily time of reading and reflection on Scripture that the word of God proclaimed to me during the Liturgy "came alive."

I also find that the words of Scripture come alive for me at various times during the day when a thought from Scripture simply comes into my mind. The Lord speaks to me through his word by bringing passages to mind—passages which are appropriate to the situation that I am in, or passages which contain a truth that I need to hear. My daily reading is still indispensable, for it provides the material that the Lord brings to my mind, and it enables me to understand the basic meaning and context of different passages from Scripture.

The important point is that we need to listen to the word of God addressed to us. Our faithful reading of Scripture plays an essential role in this, even on days when the words seem to lie lifeless on the page. The Lord will use our faithful reading in a variety of ways: to prepare us to hear him speak to us in other ways later that day; to prepare us to listen to his word during the Liturgy; to provide our minds with a passage that he will later have us recall with insight or application in a particular situation. In our reading, we enter into the world of Scripture so that the word of God may break into our world and our lives.

Not every book in the Bible will speak to us equally clearly, or be equally enlightening to us. We should not be afraid to admit to ourselves that there is much in the Bible that we do not understand, and that does not seem to speak to our situation. It is no disgrace if we find Leviticus less nourishing than the Gospel of John. It is to be expected that the Lord will speak a word of guidance more frequently through Paul's letters than through the Book of Daniel. One does not find every book in a library equally helpful or interesting at every moment—or even ever.

While God wishes to speak with us on a daily basis, we can expect his voice to be loudest and most distinct at the turning points and critical junctures of our lives. When we are most in need of guidance and assurance, we should have the greatest expectation of hearing the Lord's voice as we prayerfully turn to him.

Scripture played a critical role in the conversion of St. Augustine. One day when he was wrestling with the Lord in prayer, wondering about the direction of his life, he heard a child's voice singing out, "Take it and read it. Take it and read it." Augustine recounts what happened in his *Confessions:*

> I checked the force of my tears and rose to my feet, being quite certain that I must interpret this as a divine command to me to open the Bible and read the first passage which I should come upon. For I had heard this about St. Anthony: he had happened to come in when the Gospel was being read, and as though the words read were spoken directly to himself had received the admonition: "Go, sell all that you have, and give to the poor, and you shall have treasure in heaven, and come and follow me." And by such a message he had been immediately converted.
>
> I snatched up the Bible, opened it, and read in silence the passage upon which my eyes first fell: "Not in reveling and drunkenness, not in debauchery and licentiousness, not in quarreling and jealousy. But put on the Lord Jesus Christ, and make no provision for the flesh, to gratify its desires." I had no wish to read further; there was no need to. For immediately I had reached the end of this sentence it was as though my heart was filled with a light of confidence and all the shadows of my doubt were swept away.   **Book VIII, Chapter 12**

That was the critical turning point in Augustine's life. He was on the road to conversion before this incident, but those words of Scripture spoke to his heart in a way that swept aside doubt and clearly indicated the path that he was to follow.

God may speak more dramatically at critical points in our lives, but we should expect that he will be present and will speak to us as a normal part of our daily reading of Scripture. Some days his voice may be more gentle than other days; some days his voice may seem to be stilled. But his voice will never be truly silent, if we but know how to listen to it and understand what he says. Some of the days on which he seems to be not saying anything he may indeed be speaking—but speaking a word we do not care to hear, or speaking in a way that we have not yet learned to recognize.

The most common word that the Lord will speak to our hearts will be a message of love, an assurance that we are loved by the Father as his children. Any number of passages in the New Testament may be the springboard for this word. We may identify ourselves with Peter's protest, "Get away from me, Lord, for I am a sinful man," and then realize that Jesus' response to Peter is the same response that he makes to our own feelings of unworthiness. The Holy Spirit may enlighten us to understand that Jesus cares about every aspect of our lives—just as he cared about such little matters as the wine running out at a marriage feast and just as he wept over the tragedy of the death of his friend, Lazarus. And the full impact of that often quoted verse, John 3:16, may come home to us: "God so loved the world that he gave his only Son, that whoever believes in him should not perish but have eternal life" (RSV). It is one thing to know in the abstract the truth of this statement; it is another thing to personally accept Jesus Christ as one's savior, and to realize that one is called to eternal life through him.

The message of Scripture is also one of invitation. Just as Jesus issued the call, "Follow me," to the first disciples, he issues it to us today. God's message of love is not something that we can simply note without allowing it to affect our lives. It is a personal invitation calling for a response. In the simplest terms, it is the invitation, "Follow me."

The call to follow Jesus is a call to imitate him. Here the invitation of Scripture gets more specific, and the word that we hear God speaking to us will often assume very definite meaning. Jesus invites us to give our entire lives over to him. After we have responded wholeheartedly to this call comes the day in, day out living in imitation of Christ. We will continue to need specific words from Jesus to guide us.

Some of the words of Jesus are outright commands—uncompromising, clear-cut commands. It is a mistake to read the Bible as if it were only a book of commandments; it is also a mistake to read it as if it contained no definite commands. The words that Jesus addresses to us through Scripture are words with authority, words demanding obedience. We must be prepared to hear them as such and to obey.

THE HOLY SPIRIT

The inspiration of the Holy Spirit is essential to our reading Scripture as the word of God. Along with our efforts to understand Scripture and our resolve to read with an open heart, the Holy Spirit must be present as we read if we are to truly listen to God speak to us through the words of Scripture and obey with an eager heart.

We are given the Holy Spirit through our baptism into Jesus Christ. The Father adopts us as his sons and daughters and allows us to partake of his very life. As children of God, we are equipped to listen to his voice. Jesus promised that his message would live on in us through the work of the Holy Spirit: "I have said these things to you while still with you; but the Advocate, the Holy Spirit, whom the Father will send in my name, will teach you everything and remind you of all I have said to you" (Jn 14:25-26 JB). The Holy Spirit fulfilled the promise made by God through the prophet Jeremiah: "This is the covenant I will make with the House of Israel when those days arrive—it is Yahweh who speaks. Deep within them I will plant my Law, writing it on their hearts. Then I will be their God and they shall be my people" (Jer 31:33 JB).

The same Holy Spirit who inspired the Old Testament prophets to speak the word of God is given to us so that the word of God may root deeply into our hearts. Jesus promised that, "When the Advocate comes, whom I shall send you from the Father, the Spirit of truth who issues from the Father, he will be my witness" (Jn 15:26 JB). It is no accident that Jesus calls the Holy Spirit the Spirit of truth. The truth that the Spirit bears witness to is the truth that through Jesus Christ we have been redeemed and made children of God: "For those who are led by the Spirit of God are children of God. For you did not receive a spirit of slavery to fall back into fear, but you received a spirit of adoption, through which we cry, '*Abba*, Father!' The Spirit itself bears witness with our spirit that we are children of God" (Rom 8:14-16 NAB).

It is through the work of the Holy Spirit that the words of Scripture come alive when we read them. Through his work within us, the words we read are not merely words, but words of life. Through his presence and power within us, we can read Scripture as the word of God, and experience those words transforming our lives.

Like any gift of the Holy Spirit, the graces we need to read Scripture properly are given in response to our prayer. If we want the help of the Holy Spirit, we must ask for it. He can certainly help us on those days when we forget to ask (fortunately he does), but it should be our firm resolve to begin our every time of Scripture reading with a prayer. Our prayer need not be lengthy or complex: it can be a simple "Come, Holy Spirit, inspire and guide me as I read the Bible today." Or it could be the prayer to the Holy Spirit, the "Come, Holy Spirit." What is important is that we express our attitude of dependence on the Holy Spirit to guide us; what is important is that we acknowledge our need for God's help in order to read Scripture as his word. Our prayer not only acknowledges our dependence; it is also an expression of our confidence that we will receive the help we need if we ask for it.

How does the help of the Holy Spirit come to us? What do his gifts and graces do within us? In my own experience of reading Scripture, I can pick out four ways the Holy Spirit helps me, four different stages of his drawing me more deeply into the truths of revelation.

First of all, *the Holy Spirit guides us to have a correct understanding of the inspired meaning of the words of Scripture.* This is not an infused grace of enlightenment that strikes us while we are passively staring into space; it is a work of the Spirit that cooperates with our own hard work in trying to understand a text. Nor does it guarantee us a correct understanding of the text; infallible guidance is given to the Church, not to us as ordinary members.

Then what is this kind of help we receive from the Spirit? I believe that it begins with the simple grace of a clear mind. For example, some days I am so tired or preoccupied that I have a hard time reading the evening newspaper with much understanding. I read through some news item, perhaps on the state of the economy, and at the end have no clear idea what I read. Sometimes I am similarly afflicted when I turn to the Bible. I read a passage, but the words seem to bounce off my mind like background music in department stores.

Reading with full attention demands that we do it when we are as alert and mentally fresh as possible. Sometimes it means making a conscious effort to put distraction out of our minds. But I also think that a clear mind is a grace of the Holy Spirit; Scripture passages only come alive for me when I am able to pay attention to what they are saying.

I find that my own understanding of the Scripture text begins with a careful reading of the text itself, with as clear and undistracted a mind as possible. I try to analyze what is happening in the text—what point Jesus or Paul or the author is making. If I find a verse bewildering, I will try to find some explanation of it in a commentary. I may reflect on other passages of Scripture which throw light on the text I am trying to understand.

What I do, in other words, is what almost anyone would do in trying to understand something they are reading, whether in the Bible or in some other book. I believe that the Holy Spirit enters into this process by guiding and cooperating with my efforts.

Sometimes I receive insights into a passage which come out of the blue, and it is easy to acknowledge them as insights from the Spirit in response to my prayer for guidance and understanding. But most often his grace works in a very gentle and unobtrusive manner, guiding my efforts rather than replacing them.

However the Holy Spirit works, the end result is what is

important. Our aim should be to have a correct understanding of the inspired meaning of the words of the Bible. When we have finished reading we should have a sense that we basically understand what we read, and perhaps even have a few new insights into its meaning. That is the first work of the Spirit in us as we read Scripture, the first stage of the guidance he gives us.

The second grace we should ask of the Spirit is that *we are able to read the Bible as God's word, to us,* a message addressed particularly to us as individuals, a message with meaning for today. This presupposes reading the Bible with understanding and builds on it.

Often after studying a passage of Scripture I will have the sense that I understand it, particularly if I have made use of commentaries and other study helps. But sometimes I will nonetheless feel that something important is missing—the meaning of the passage *for me.* It is as if I understand many things about the passage, but still do not grasp its point for my life.

For example, the last time I read the Gospel of John I learned many things about the episode of the woman caught in the act of adultery (Jn 8:1-11). I found out that scholars are almost unanimous in agreeing that this passage was written by someone other than John and that it was a late addition to the Gospel. In reading the passage I noticed what might have been a "double standard": why wasn't the man who was caught in the same sin also hauled before Jesus, since the law prescribed the same penalty for him? I turned to the Old Testament laws on adultery and read them as background. I noted the self-righteousness of the scribes and Pharisees, and that their real intent was to put Jesus on the spot rather than to uphold the law. I found out that scholars do not know what Jesus wrote on the ground, and do not even have any theories which struck me as likely.

I noted many other details about the passage, and read many other scholarly conclusions about it. I was able to re-create the episode quite vividly in my imagination. But I still had little sense of what the message of the passage was for me. If this event had been omitted from the Bible, my own spiritual life would have been little poorer at this point.

It was only after prayer and further reflection that some messages for me began to emerge. I began to see that in my own relationship with Jesus, I stood in the place of the woman. I have sinned; I have transgressed the laws of God. Jesus does not pretend that I am not a sinner (just as he did not tell the woman, "It was really okay for you to commit adultery, as long as it was a meaningful experience"). But neither does Jesus look on my sin as the opportunity to condemn me that he had been waiting for. There is a sadness in his eyes that I have sinned, but also a gentleness. There is a strength in his words to me, "Do not sin any more," and also hope.

Another message for me also came through this passage. I saw myself in the place of the scribes and Pharisees with regard to my own children. How often have I upheld the law primarily to demonstrate my own righteousness rather than out of concern for them? How often have I been harsh and inconsiderate of their feelings, even when their conduct called for correction? How often have I been quick to condemn but failed to give them the patient attention that would help them grow in the way of true maturity and righteousness?

Sometimes the word of God from Scripture that is addressed to me is not by way of example, as in this case, but by a more direct word. It is one thing to read John 15:16 and understand that Jesus is telling the apostles that he had chosen them; it is another thing to hear those words spoken from all eternity to oneself: "You did not choose me, no, I chose you."

If the words of Scripture are to come alive to us as a here-and-now communication of God's word to us, then the power of the Spirit must fill those words, transforming them from being dead squiggles of ink on a page to being words spoken now, addressed to us by name. If our application of the words of Scripture to our lives is to be rooted in this inspired meaning of the text, then we need the guidance of the Spirit to preserve us from arbitrary interpretations and error. If what we read is to have the power to transform us, then the transforming power of the Spirit must be at work within us, for only the Spirit has the power to give life and growth. And that is the second work and grace of the Spirit that we should pray for as we read the Bible.

The third aspect of the Spirit's work within us as we read

Scripture is a little harder for me to describe, but I think none-theless quite real and very important: *the Holy Spirit gives us insight into the mysteries of God which Scripture reveals.* In the words of the Second Vatican Council, "Through divine revelation, God chose to show forth and communicate himself" ("Divine Revelation," section 6). Scripture does not merely contain facts about God, even facts that we have a sense are personally important for us. Scripture contains something of God's revelation of *himself,* a revelation that is of necessity the revelation of a mystery.

Again an example might help. The opening verses of John's Gospel can be studied for their meaning and poetic structure. They can be examined for their message for us today. But these words point to great mysteries: the mystery of the Word of God existing from the beginning; the mystery of all things being created through his Word; the mystery of this Word becoming flesh and dwelling among us. If these words do not arouse wonder and awe in us, we are only skimming the surface of their meaning. If these words do not lead us into contemplation of the mysteries of the Trinity and the incarnation, then we are missing much of the revelation of himself that God intends to give us through these words.

Our limited human understanding is woefully inadequate in the face of the mysteries of God, even our understanding aided by study and the normal graces of the Holy Spirit. Now we can see only a dim reflection of the glory of God, as if in a clouded mirror. But the Holy Spirit can give us momentary graces, special glimpses of the reality of God. The Holy Spirit can cause words of Scripture that we have read many times to suddenly stun us with the truth they tell us about God.

Such graces cannot be forced; they can only be gratefully received. But they can be prayed for. We can ask the Spirit to unveil our minds as we read Scripture so that in the words of the Bible we encounter the one who spoke them. We can ask that God's word to us be a revelation of himself, and not merely truths about himself. We can ask that we receive the grace of being drawn up into the mysteries of God, the gift of a fleeting glimpse of his face.

If we receive such a grace of the Holy Spirit, we will find ourselves naturally drawn to prayer. But even if our reading of Scripture does not draw us to such heights, it should lead to and nourish our prayer, and this is the fourth work of the Holy Spirit in us: *the Spirit inspires our response to God in prayer.* He moves our wills to accept what we read and submit in obedience to it; he moves our hearts to respond in joy to God. He gives words to us to express our response; he gives us the wordless sense of God's presence. If our reading of Scripture is truly an encounter with the God who reveals himself through its words, then our response naturally and inevitably has to be prayer. And as we soon find out, prayer which is not graced by the Holy Spirit can be dry and difficult indeed. Hence we need the help of the Spirit if we are to respond as we should to the word we read.

The Holy Spirit can work in us in very quiet ways. When I first began to read the Bible in a daily and serious way some years ago, I began each reading with a brief prayer that the Lord would speak to me through the words that I read. It was a simple informal prayer, but a prayer that I never omitted. At first my reading of Scripture was merely interesting; it had a freshness because I had never before seriously studied the Bible and so was reading many passages for the first time. But one day, after months of daily reading, I became aware that I was reading Scripture on a different level than when I began. I was reading it as God's word to me, not merely as an interesting book. I became aware that in my reading the Lord was speaking to me—about himself, about myself, about my life with him.

I realized then that my prayer was being answered: that the Lord was speaking to me as I read. I also realized that he had been doing this for some time—at least several months. His voice had come so gently that I hadn't been aware of it. He had not answered my prayer by a voice abruptly thundering from the heavens; he had answered it by gradual degrees, quietly, peacefully. If I had been more alert, I would no doubt have noticed it sooner.

What I experienced then was the work of the Holy Spirit within me. It was not an emotion; it was not a startling revelation; it was rarely dramatic. But my heart *did* burn within me as

I read the words of Scripture, and I read even familiar passages with a new understanding and a new insight into their meaning for me. I had begun reading Scripture because I knew it was a good thing to do; now I read eagerly, with a hunger and thirst for the word of God. I had begun reading Scripture because it contained the word of God; now I experienced that it contained words of God addressed directly to me, speaking to my daily experience of following Christ.

To me, this grace was given gradually. Others have experienced more sudden and dramatic workings of the Holy Spirit within them, drawing them to the pages of Scripture with an overwhelming attraction, making the words of Scripture come alive to them as never before. The very suddenness with which this gift can be given testifies to the power of the Holy Spirit. It is he who makes the words come alive; it is he who inflames our hearts with eagerness to read and obey; it is he who enlightens our minds so that we understand what we read.

This work of the Holy Spirit is a gift; we cannot attain it by ourselves, no matter how hard we try or how much we strain. Our hearts won't burn within us as we read simply because we wish that they would. We can only carry out our part, and pray for him to do his part. Our part is to be faithful in our reading, serious in our study, and pray for the inspiration of the Holy Spirit. The rest is up to him and we can rely on him to do his part. He may act gradually, as he did in my life. He may act dramatically, as he has done in the lives of some of my friends. But faithful to the promises of Jesus, the Holy Spirit will be with us if we ask, and will equip us to read Scripture as the word of God. "If you then, who are evil, know how to give good gifts to your children, how much more will the heavenly Father give the Holy Spirit to those who ask him!" (Lk 11:13 RSV).

WORDS OF LIFE

"Then he said to them all, 'If any want to become my followers, let them deny themselves and take up their cross daily and follow me. For those who want to save their life will lose it, and those who lose their life for my sake will save it. What does it profit them if they gain the whole world, but lose or forfeit themselves?" (Lk 9:23-25 NRSV).

We can read these words in several ways. We may read them in a very general and impersonal sense, as a law of cause and effect: if anyone does this, then that happens. We can understand what the words mean and nod agreement, much as we would to the sentence, "If anyone drops a rubber ball on a concrete floor, it will bounce." However, that kind of reading would give these words of Jesus no more meaning for our lives than the words about the bouncing properties of a rubber ball.

These words can also be understood as a command: "Thou shalt renounce thyself and take up the cross." We can even acknowledge that in some sense we are to obey this command—along with many other commands and laws: "Thou shalt pay thy income taxes by April 15 of each year." While this brings the words of Jesus one step closer to us, we are still not truly hearing those words as his words to us. Reading the Bible merely as a book of commands, as a book of do's and don'ts, is still not reading the Scripture as the word of God.

We can, finally, read these words as the word of God to us and for us. We might read them as if they were addressed to us by name: "Then to George Martin, Jesus said: 'If you want to be a follower of mine, renounce yourself and your own desires, take up your cross every day and follow me. If you try to preserve your own life, you will lose it. But if you expend your life for my sake, without worrying about yourself, then you will find true life. What gain would it be for you, George, to become wealthy and free of responsibilities, but to ruin yourself in the process?'"

When we listen to the words of Scripture as God speaking to us, we must listen to them in the concrete situation of our lives. To "take up our cross and follow Jesus" is not just a nice general metaphor; it refers to following the path for our lives that Jesus reveals to us and asks of us, and bearing whatever difficulties and sacrifices that path entails. It means not letting the trials and difficulties make us turn back from the way that the Lord wants us to walk.

This path will be unique for each one of us. Jesus will reveal his will for us in a variety of ways, often simply through circumstances. Quite often the problem is not in determining what the path of Jesus is for us, but in resolving to follow it once we know it. Then these words of Jesus will have their full force and meaning: "If any want to become my followers, let them deny themselves."

Since each of our life situations is different, the specific meaning of these words of Jesus will be different for us. We may be facing a choice of taking one job rather than another, knowing that the lower paying job would be of greater service to the Lord. We may have an opportunity to take a homeless person into our house, but know that this would call for some sacrifice, perhaps loss of privacy, perhaps additional financial burden. We may have the opportunity to move to a better climate, but have retired parents dependent upon us where we are living now.

In most cases, taking one course rather than another would not be a matter of sin. But it is often clear which choice would be the choice of following after Jesus and imitating him as a servant. In these situations, our reading of Scripture will let God speak to us and our concrete situation in very specific terms. God's words to us then will not be merely abstract truths or general commands. They will be words of consolation in the specific choice that is made: "If anyone loses his or her life for my sake [by providing a home for one of my children who needs it], that person will find it." They will be words of promise, specifically addressed to us: "If you choose now not the easier path, but the more difficult path that I am calling you to follow, you will paradoxically have chosen the way that is best for you." They will be words that put our life and choices in perspective: "What gain is it for you to have everything the way you want it here and now, but to have forsaken my path and my calling?" The words of Jesus are words of life; the call of Jesus is a call to eternal life.

Jesus addresses to us the same words he spoke when he walked on earth: "Listen, anyone who has ears to hear!" He tells us that "a child of God listens to the words of God" (Jn 8:47 JB). He invites us to listen to his words, to let his words come alive in our lives.

A woman who was deaf from birth might find the musical score to a Beethoven symphony in the library and become fascinated by it. She could spend hours studying it, even memorize the way the written notes followed one upon the other. She could read books about music and the laws of harmony. But because of her deafness, she would never truly experience and understand the greatness of Beethoven's symphony. For Beethoven did not primarily write notes; he created music—a living reality only dimly captured in the written score. Music exists only in the performance and hearing.

God's word to us only truly exists as it is addressed to us and listened to by us. The words of Scripture can be dead words if we do not have ears to listen to them. They can have as little life for us as the symphony score would have for the deaf woman: something that we read and study, but never understand. The words of Scripture must come alive in our lives if they are to be the word of God for us. If we allow them to, then we will find that they are truly words of life.

Because Jesus Christ has redeemed us, we can turn to the Father and ask that the Holy Spirit be manifestly active in us, prompting us to read the words of Scripture with reverence and love, giving us wisdom and insight to understand them, guiding us in applying them to our own lives, strengthening us to gladly respond in faith and obedience. We can pray with confidence that the Word of God will speak to us through the words of the Bible. We can have confidence that in answer to our prayer, he will speak not only to our minds, but also to our hearts.

For Christians, it is an article of belief that the Bible is unlike any other book, that it contains the words of God to the human race. For one who reads the Bible as the word of God, this is a matter of experience. Those who read the words of Scripture under the guidance and inspiration of the Holy Spirit can truly say that God does speak to them and call them by name: "You have come to God himself, the supreme Judge, and been placed with spirits of the saints who have been made perfect; and to Jesus, the mediator who brings a new covenant.... Make sure that you never refuse to listen when he speaks" (Heb 12:23-24, 25 JB).

FOUR

Praying

When the angels had gone from them into heaven, the shepherds said to one another, "Let us go to Bethlehem and see this thing that has happened which the Lord has made known to us." So they hurried away and found Mary and Joseph, and the baby lying in the manger. When they saw the child they repeated what they had been told about him, and everyone who heard it was astonished at what the shepherds had to say.   for Mary, she treasured all these things and pondered them in her heart.

Luke 2:15-19 JB

T HE EVENTS SURROUNDING THE BIRTH of Jesus into the world were not so simple as our Christmas cribs may lull us into thinking. Because we are so familiar with the opening pages of the Gospels of Luke and Matthew we may think that we understand all there is to understand about Jesus' birth. But if we reread those familiar passages slowly and thoughtfully, we will find much to reflect on.

What a great act of faith was required of Joseph! What feelings and thoughts must have run through his mind! He knew Mary to be a very good woman, a very holy, prayerful woman. But when "she was found to be with child through the Holy Spirit" (Mt 1:18 JB)—through the Spirit of the Lord whom they adored—what great strength from the Holy Spirit he himself must have received to accept that fact, to accept that the Lord had chosen the woman that he had chosen, to believe that this child was the Son of God. Joseph's faith in God and in his wife-to-be was firm and his love for them was total, but it still was a faith and love that did not fully understand the things that were happening. For who could understand that the Son of God would be born into the world, not in might and splendor, but off in the hills and laid in a manger? Who was this Son of God, that he chose to come in such a way?

When the shepherds heard the angels' message, "they were terrified" (Lk 2:9 JB). What did the words of the angels mean? The messiah that the chosen people expected was to be an earthly king, one who would recapture for them the kingdom of David from the Romans. The Book of Isaiah had told them differently; it told of the coming of the Lord's suffering servant who would bear their sins. This was the Christ that the shepherds found in the manger, one in whom "there was in him no stately bearing to make us look at him, nor appearance that would attract us to him" (Is 53:2 NAB). On the one hand, the glorious appearance of the angels; on the other hand, a child born in poverty.

"As for Mary, she treasured all these things, and pondered them in her heart." She too must have been unable to fully comprehend all that was happening. She knew that the Lord was indeed at work, that what was happening was part of his plan of salvation. But to know that God's hand is guiding us is not the same as understanding all that he is doing. Mary's faith, her love of God, her "behold the handmaid of the Lord; let his will be done in me" was never diminished. But there was still the need to treasure the events of Christ's coming into the world and into her life, and ponder them in her heart. And in treasuring those events in her heart, she provides a model for us in our prayerful use of Scripture.

We usually think of prayer as words we say, whether they be the set prayers that we learned as children or the informal prayers that come from our heart. Words are indeed one aspect of our prayer, but they must be based on and a result of a more primary contact with God. In our ordinary life, we must be with a friend before we can speak to a friend. So too in our conversation with God: we must be in his presence, listening to him as well as speaking to him, if we are to pray properly. Reading Scripture can play an important part in coming into his presence and listening to him. For most of us, reading Scripture each day will be the best springboard to prayer that we have available. And Mary provides us with a model in this.

The Gospels do not record Mary saying very much. They do record her being present in the background throughout our Lord's life. She was present at the wedding feast at Cana, when, according to John's Gospel, Jesus worked his first sign. She was present at the foot of the cross. She was present when the Holy Spirit fell on those assembled in the upper room on Pentecost day. She was not called to publicly proclaim the good news, nor to heal the sick or work wonders. Her call was simply to be present, and to treasure the events of Jesus' life in her heart. Even when the actions of Jesus baffled her or caused her pain—as they did when he stayed behind in Jerusalem at the age of twelve— she "stored up all these things in her heart" (Lk 2:52 JB).

Being in the presence of Jesus and treasuring his words in our hearts is the first step of prayer. It is also the first fruit of our reading Scripture: we are simply there, as it was, while the saving plan of God unfolds through Abraham and Moses and the prophets, and finally through Jesus. Our reading, our study, and especially our listening to the word of God as it speaks to us through the pages of Scripture are meant to give us a treasure that we can hold in our hearts.

In pondering the events of Jesus' life, Mary was not merely thinking them over. We think things over when they are detached from us and don't affect us very much. Still less did she brood over what was happening—as we sometimes find ourselves doing when our lives do not seem to be going the way we feel they should. Mary's pondering was a reflection on events that affected her deeply—a faith-filled reflection which knew that the hand of God was present in every situation, even when she did not fully understand God's plan. She knew that what was happening was happening because of God's love for his people and for her—and in her heart she both treasured that love and returned it. Her reflection was an attempt to more fully respond and enter into the mystery that she had been called to live.

And in this light we can glimpse a fuller meaning of Jesus' words about his mother: "He was told, 'Your mother and your brothers are standing outside and want to see you.' But he said in answer, 'My mother and my brothers are those who hear the word of God and put it into practice'" (Lk 8:20-21 JB). "Now as he was speaking, a woman in the crowd raised her voice and said, 'Happy the womb that bore you and the breasts you sucked!' But he replied, 'Still happier those who hear the word of God and keep it!'" (Lk 11:27-28 JB). These words were no rejection of Mary if she was indeed the one who heard the invitation of God through Gabriel and responded to it, if she was indeed the one who witnessed the events and words of Jesus and kept them in her heart. What the Holy Spirit did in her at the conception of Jesus and what he continued to do throughout her life were of far more importance than the mere biological fact of motherhood.

Just as Mary kept all these things in her heart, so we are called to keep the word of God that has been addressed to us, "meditating on it day and night" (Jos 1:8 JB).

KEEPING THE WORD

"If anyone loves me he will keep my word, and my Father will love him, and we shall come to him and make our home with him" (Jn 14:23 JB). We usually understand this verse to be a repetition of verse fifteen of chapter fourteen of John's Gospel: "If you love me you will keep my commandments." Obedience is certainly a part of "keeping the word" of Jesus. However, there is also a deeper meaning to "keeping the word."

Jesus made a promise to his followers: "If you continue in my word, you are truly my disciples, and you will know the truth, and the truth will make you free" (Jn 8:31-32 RSV). The meaning would seem to be: "If you continue to listen to my word and take it to heart, you will be doing something that is truly necessary in order to be my disciple. I will reveal the truth to those who yearn to hear my word, and the truth that I will reveal to them will set them on the right path, giving them true freedom."

In contrast to the disciples, those who rejected Jesus rejected his word. Jesus told them that at the root of their desire to kill him was a rejection of the word that he was addressing to them: "You seek to kill me because my word finds no place in you" (Jn 8:37 RSV). The Jerusalem Bible translates the last part of this verse, "because nothing I say has penetrated into you."

The contrast is clear: involved in a rejection of Jesus is a rejection of his word, a refusal to listen to it and let it penetrate into our hearts. Part of following Jesus is listening for his word, desiring to be formed by his word, constantly meditating on his word, keeping his word in our hearts and minds, obeying his word. Those who "keep the word" of Jesus are those who do let it penetrate into them and transform them.

We are promised that "if you make my word your home you will indeed be my disciples" (Jn 8:31 JB). The image here is of living in the word of Jesus as we would in our family home: a familiar place of security that we can always return to, a place where we love and are loved, a place that provides roots in a world that sometimes perplexes or wearies us. The image of God's word as our home carries notions of intimacy and familiarity; it carries the notion that the word of God is our primary place of rootedness in a world of change, a world that is passing away.

Keeping the word of God in our hearts, making the word of God our home, letting the word of God penetrate into us—this is the first step of prayer. The transition from reading and listening to praying is not an abrupt one. As we read with reverence the words of the Bible, we in fact begin to pray. When we read a psalm properly, we read it as a prayer. When we listen to the words that Jesus addresses to his Father in chapter seventeen of John's Gospel, we enter into them as our prayer also, joining with Christ in asking the Father that we be one with him and all Christians, asking that we be consecrated to the truth. When we marvel at God's love for us, treasuring it in our hearts, our attitude is that of Paul exclaiming, "How rich are the depths of God—how deep his wisdom and knowledge" (Rom 11:33 JB), and this exclamation is a prayer.

Scripture is not only God's word to us; it is also our speaking with God under his inspiration. The Bible is not a one-way communication from God to us; it is also a part of our communication with God. This communication begins when we listen to God and treasure his words in our hearts—that very treasuring becomes our prayer.

The Second Vatican Council taught: "Prayer should accompany the reading of Scripture, so that God and man talk together; for we speak to Him when we pray; we hear Him when we read the divine sayings" ("Divine Revelation," Section 25).

Although the transition from reading Scripture to prayer is a gradual one, prayer is different from our usual Scripture reading. In our regular daily reading time, we concentrate on understanding Scripture text and on listening to God's word in the words of the Bible. In prayer we enter into conversation with God, using our own words or the words of Scripture to express the thoughts of our hearts.

Besides the time we spend reading Scripture, then, we need to take time for personal prayer, our communication with God. Many people—myself included—like to set aside time for prayer immediately after their time for Scripture reading, so that the word they have heard in their reading can become the basis for their conversation with God. Others prefer to separate reading and prayer times. But however they are scheduled, it is important that we allow times for both reading and prayer. We should not skimp on one for the sake of the other.

Previous chapters have given advice on ways to use a daily time for reading Scripture. I would like now to suggest ways we can use Scripture to enrich the time we spend with God in prayer. Just as we need to resolve to spend a certain amount of time each day with the Bible in order to make reading it a part of our lives, so we will need to take certain steps in order to truly keep the word of God in our hearts and respond in prayer. Two methods we can use are to pray with Scripture and to pray the words of Scripture. There is nothing sacred about the steps or approaches I will outline, but they have been found helpful by many people in making the transition from reading to praying.

PRAYING WITH THE BIBLE

One successful way to use Scripture in prayer is to follow the ancient Christian tradition of "reading, thinking, praying": we first read a portion from Scripture, then think about it, then respond to God in prayer. In practice these steps become interwoven; they are not three stages so much as three aspects of what we do when we read Scripture to nourish our prayer.

It may be more helpful to think of the steps or aspects as "reading, reflecting, listening, conversing, adoring." Again, these are not mutually exclusive acts, but different facets of a prayerful use of Scripture. We read—but read reflectively, pondering what is said. We listen to God speak to us through the words of Scripture, applying them to our own lives. We enter into conversation with Christ, responding with love to the love that he has for us, talking with Jesus as we would with a friend. But our talking with Jesus is different than merely talking with a friend; he is the Christ, the Son of God, and our response to him must also be adoration. Perhaps our adoration takes the form of a prayer of thanksgiving, perhaps the form of a prayer of praise, or perhaps it is not expressed in words at all, but is the silent adoration of our hearts in his presence.

It was said earlier that our every reading of Scripture should begin with prayer—at least the simple prayer, "Speak, Lord, for your servant is listening" (1 Sm 3:9 NAB). Since it is the Holy Spirit who comes to our aid in prayer and inspires us to pray (Rom 8:26-27), we should begin our praying with Scripture by invoking his presence and help.

We particularly should make an effort to place ourselves in the presence of God. If we must be alone with God to listen to him speaking to us through the words of Scripture, we must also be alone with him in order to respond to his speaking with our prayer. Being alone with God does not mean ignoring our problems or trying by sheer willpower to put preoccupations out of our minds. It means bringing them to God, laying them at his feet, and letting go of them. Our focus must be on him, not on our problems or distractions. If we do this, we will be able to view our problems in his light, through his perspective. We will be able to listen to him speak to our problems because we are more intent on listening to him than we are on worrying about them.

Nor does being alone with God mean that we must shut ourselves off from other people. We can be in his presence while praying in the midst of a group of people; on the other hand, we can be shut in our closet and have our minds far from him. To be alone with God means to put ourselves fully in his presence, whether we are praying by ourselves or with others.

Thus, our initial prayer should be a prayer that we can truly be in God's presence. It should be a prayer that the Holy Spirit will draw us into being alone with God, attentive to his word, able to respond with love to the love that he has for us. We should not demand of ourselves that we achieve some instant mystical state, but neither should we neglect this prayer; it is better to spend a few extra minutes in preparation than to rush into our prayer time with distractions in the forefront of our minds.

As we turn from our opening prayer to actually praying with the Scripture, several approaches are possible, although they all accomplish the same purpose and have many features in common.

One approach is to read a passage from the Bible, then reflect upon it, and enter into a conversation with Christ based on our reading and reflection. The reading might be a passage or chapter from that day's regular Scripture reading, particularly if we are reading from the New Testament. Or it might be specially chosen for prayer—perhaps from the Gospels—particularly if we are reading from the Old Testament in our regular reading time and find difficulty in using it as the basis of prayer.

The amount we read should not be great—perhaps only a few paragraphs. We want something to be the basis of reflection and prayer; we are not reading to get a first acquaintance with a chapter or to survey a whole book of Scripture. After carefully reading the passage we have chosen, we reflect on it, savor it, absorb it into our minds and hearts, and listen to what the Lord may be saying to us through it. This then can be the subject matter of our prayer, our conversation with Christ. More will be said about the conversation aspect of our prayer a little later.

Another approach is to make reading itself our prayer, our conversation with Christ. This calls for very slow reading that allows us to linger over every verse, sometimes over every word. We read a verse, reflect on it, listen to the word of God speaking to us through it, and respond to him from our hearts. We only move on to the next verse when we have extracted all the meaning that we can from the first, and have turned it over in our hearts in the presence of God.

With this approach, there will be no set amount that we plan to read. If we are reading a passage that does not speak very forcefully to our hearts, we may find that at the end of our prayer time we have covered a sizeable amount of Scripture— because none of it provided us with very much material for reflection and prayer that day. On other days, perhaps when we are using a different book from Scripture, we may find that our entire prayer time is taken up with reflecting on a single verse and praying through all the insights we receive from it.

Whichever approach we use, we must keep uppermost in our minds that we are reading and praying in order to enter more fully into the life of Christ. We are not trying to cover a certain amount of Scripture; we are not trying to achieve a perfect prayer that passes all the tests of prayer. We will have good days and bad days; we will experience dryness and frustration, and also experience the manifest presence of God, wooing our hearts as he wooed the heart of ancient Israel. What is important is our faithfulness, our attitude of heart in turning toward him, our opening of ourselves to the power of the Holy Spirit. Beyond that, the insights we receive and the depths of prayer that we experience are gifts of the Holy Spirit, subject to his control, not ours.

The approach that I use most often in praying from the Scripture combines the two approaches described above. I usually base my prayer on the passage that I am reading for that day—usually a chapter in the book that I am working my way through. As I read during my regular reading time, I mark in the margin any verses that strike me as likely to provide food for reflection and application to my own life. Should any verse immediately speak to me as if it were the Lord speaking to me, I of course mark it (and sometimes go immediately to prayer, preferring to finish up my regular reading later on).

When I have finished my set reading, I turn to prayer and go back over the verses I've marked, one by one, using them as material for reflection. I listen to what the Lord may wish to say to me through them, making them the basis of my prayer. My experience is that there is usually something, even in the driest passages of Scripture, that will strike my mind in a fresh way and provide food for prayer. If one marked passage doesn't provide enough basis for prayer, I turn to another one. Sometimes, though, the first passage provides ample material for my prayer time, as I trace and retrace its message and implication for me, as I apply it to my life, as I let it sink into my heart as the word of God.

There is one danger in all of these approaches to praying with Scripture: our prayer time might become merely a time of Scripture reading. However necessary it is to read Scripture, it is also necessary to pray. Our prayer can often be best made as a response to the Scripture that we have read and reflected on. But our reading of Scripture and our study of Scripture should never replace our turning to God in prayer and conversing with him. If we find we are spending more and more of our prayer time reading Scripture, we should take appropriate means to restore the balance. Perhaps the Lord does want us to read Scripture more, but he most likely doesn't want that additional reading to be done at the expense of our prayer.

It is important, then, that our reading lead into prayer or become prayer. We read about Christ in Scripture as a "him"; we address him in our prayers as a "you." We do not merely read about him; we converse with him, one person to another. St. Teresa of Avila defined prayer simply as a heart-to-heart conversation with him who loves us, and added that prayer does not consist in thinking much but loving much. These insights provide the basis for prayer based on Scripture.

Our reading and reflecting has given us the subject matter of our conversation with Christ. If we read the parable of the prodigal son one day, for example, our prayer that day could focus on our own sinfulness, on our need for continual forgiveness. We could express to Christ our desire to love him and our sorrow at not loving him perfectly. We could ask him for the strength to make a fresh beginning, to return again to our Father's house. We could express gratitude that our Father does search the horizon for us, waiting to welcome us home again. We could rejoice that he would kill the prize calf for us to welcome us home, and that he did not hesitate to send his own Son so that we might have forgiveness and life.

The Scripture that we read, the inspirations that we are given by the Holy Spirit, and our own needs will determine the type of prayer conversation we will have. Some passages lend themselves most to rejoicing in God's love, thanking him for it. Other passages rather bluntly present the cost of discipleship—the call to lay down our lives—and may move us to prostrate ourselves in submission to God.

Whatever passage we read, the two keys to our conversation have been given by St. Teresa: our prayer should be simple but heartfelt conversation, informal and unpretentious, and it should be characterized more by our love than by the cleverness of our thought or expression. It is the response we make to listening to the word of God speak to us through the words of Scripture.

Our conversation does not have to use many words, or ultimately words at all. We may be moved to burst into praise of God, thanking him for his love for us, rejoicing that he is God and has called us to himself, praising him simply for being himself. If we feel like bursting into song, we shouldn't think it in any way improper to do so. We may be led by the Holy Spirit in our prayer: "The Spirit too comes to help us in our weakness. For when we cannot choose words in order to pray properly, the Spirit himself expresses our plea in a way that could never be put into words, and God who knows everything in our hearts knows perfectly well what he means, and that the pleas of the saints expressed by the Spirit are according to the mind of God" (Rom 8:26-27 JB). Here the charismatic gift of praying in tongues becomes a most welcome help in giving expression to the inexpressible longings of our heart to offer praise to God.

Our conversation may equally well end in silence: in awe before the presence of God, in peaceful resting in his loving care for us. The saints have taught us that a high form of prayer is wordless: simply being in God's presence, inflamed by his Spirit within us. This may be an occasional experience for many of us—something that we cannot achieve by our own efforts, but must receive as a gift sent by God. Both shouts of praise and quietly being at the feet of Jesus are worthy forms of prayer, and worthy conclusions to our prayer which springs from Scripture. Jesus welcomed the shouts of the crowd, saying that if they were silenced the stones would shout out, and he welcomed Mary sitting simply at his feet in silence, listening to his words.

PRAYING THE WORDS OF SCRIPTURE

Another way our prayer can be enriched and augmented by Scripture is to pray the prayers that are in the Bible, making them a regular part of our prayer life.

When the apostles asked Jesus to teach them how to pray, he taught them the prayer that we know as the "Our Father." We are so familiar with it that we most often say it without reflecting on what we are saying and without fully meaning what we pray. It would pay to make the Our Father a text that we meditate on periodically, dwelling on the meaning of every word and then praying it slowly and consciously. Even the first two words—"Our Father"—are so full of meaning that they could be the basis of much reflection and conversation with God.

But the Our Father is not the only prayer in the New Testament. The Book of Revelation contains prayers offered by the saints and angels in John's vision of heaven. They express the inestimable majesty of God, and are prayers of profound adoration and praise: "Holy, holy, holy is the Lord God Almighty, he who was, and who is, and who is to come" (Rv 4:8 NAB). Some of Paul's letters apparently quote hymns that were sung in the early Church. Philippians 2:6-11 is perhaps the most notable of these hymns; Colossians 1:15-20 is another.

The Old Testament too contains prayers. Moses' song of victory after having passed through the Red Sea (Ex 15:1-18) is the first of many canticles sung to express the glory of God and to thank him for his saving acts. These prayers are scattered throughout the books of the Old Testament; some modern translations of the Bible indent them to make it obvious that they are hymns of praise.

But above all, the prayers of the Bible are the Psalms. They grew out of the life of worship of the chosen people; many of them were explicitly composed to be sung in the temple. They were written over the course of perhaps eight centuries, and reflect the changing fortunes of the Israelites during that time. Some are hymns of praise; some thank God for deliverance from enemies. Others are prayers of desolation, begging God for deliverance, wondering how long it will be before he intervenes to save his people once again. They were originally meant to be sung; we no longer possess the music and have them only in the form of poetry.

The Psalms were the prayers that Jesus and his followers used. For example, on the night before his passion "after psalms had been sung they left for the Mount of Olives" (Mt 26:30 JB). They were the prayers of the early Church: "Sing the words and tunes of the psalms and hymns when you are together, and go on singing and chanting to the Lord in your hearts" (Eph 5:19 JB). "With gratitude in your hearts sing psalms and hymns and inspired songs to God" (Col 3:16 JB). "If anyone is feeling happy, he should sing a psalm" (Jas 5:13 JB).

We should make an effort to make the Psalms our prayers.

They are an inspired form of prayer: inspired by the Holy Spirit, who is the necessary inspiration in all prayer. They have been the prayers of those that God calls to himself from the time of David to the present, and have been favored by the Church since the time of Christ.

We may find some of the Psalms difficult to pray. Some express sentiments that we would hesitate to make our own: self-righteousness, contempt for one's enemies. It's doubtful that many of us could simply pray, "May red-hot embers rain down on them, may they be flung into the abyss for good" (Ps 140:10 JB). While this is an extreme example, it is certain that some of the Psalms are less likely to express the thoughts of our hearts in prayer than others.

The important thing is that many of the Psalms express very well what we do want to express in our prayer. The first time I prayed my way through the one hundred fifty psalms, I marked the ones that readily appealed to me, and found I had checked slightly over half of them. Since then I've grown to like some of those I didn't check that first time through. To be sure, I don't find that each psalm that I like expresses my every mood in prayer. Some of the Psalms are most appropriate for confession of sin and asking of forgiveness; Psalm 51 is my favorite of these. Other psalms are better for expressing our praise, and still others our cry for help. If our prayer has its seasons, there is likely a psalm suited to its every mood.

The first step in praying the Psalms is to become familiar with them and grow in our understanding of each of them. We should initially read them and study them as we would any other part of Scripture. They should be studied as we study poems—for they are poetry. We may want to try different translations to see which captures the rhythm and imagery that best speaks to us. Once we are familiar with the Psalms and have a basic understanding of them, we can begin using them in our prayer. Perhaps we will want to begin our prayer time by reciting a psalm; perhaps we will prefer to have a storehouse of favorite psalms to end our prayers with, drawing upon the one that best sums up and expresses the way our prayer has gone that day.

Here the great variety to be found in the Psalms works to our benefit.

THE FRUIT OF PRAYER

Christ has called us to union with God. We are called to mature in the image of Christ, growing daily in the life of the Holy Spirit within us and expressing that life in love and service of others. The purpose of prayer is this union with God, this transformation of our life into the image of Christ. Prayer based on Scripture should particularly have this result, since our reading will keep our goal ever before our eyes.

Our prayer must be a true "seeking of the Lord." It is possible to use the words of Scripture as a shield against confronting Jesus face-to-face and acknowledging his lordship: "You study the Scriptures, believing that in them you have eternal life; now these same Scriptures testify to me, and yet you refuse to come to me for life" (Jn 5:39-40 JB). So our reading and prayer must not be merely a matter of listening to words and using words, but an acknowledgment of the living presence of Christ and a turning of our hearts to him in love. Jesus' invitation, "Follow me," is not merely an invitation to a certain way of life or an invitation to live by high moral standards; it is first of all an invitation to enter into a personal relationship with him. The basis of Christianity is following not a *what*, but a *whom*, a person, Jesus Christ.

Daily prayer based on reading Scripture as the word of God should also help us connect the lofty aim of union with God with the day in, day out events of our life. If we are listening correctly, we should hear God gently speak to us about the concrete concerns of life and the very specific situations in which he is calling us to love. John pointed out that if we cannot love our brother or sister whom we do see, we can scarcely claim to love God whom we cannot see (1 Jn 4:20). Proper Scripture reading should keep our prayer down to earth, so that it can be truly heaven directed.

At the same time, "here we have no lasting city; we are seeking one which is to come" (Heb 13:14 NAB). Our prayer must come to grips with the mystery of God and enter into ever fuller knowledge of him. For the saints of the Church, the way of prayer was the way in which knowing and loving finally became the same thing, a preparation for that day in which they would see God face-to-face. Paul prayed that the Christians at Ephesus would grow into a complete knowledge of God: "May the God of our Lord Jesus Christ, the Father of glory, give you a spirit of wisdom and perception of what is revealed, to bring you to a full knowledge of him. May he enlighten the eyes of your mind, so that you can see what hope his call holds for you, what rich glories he has promised the saints will inherit, and how infinitely great is the power that he has exercised for us believers" (Eph 1:17-19 JB). Note that Paul's prayer hinges on "what is revealed"; our path to a full knowledge of God must be guided by his revelation of himself. We must seek his revelation in Scripture in order to prayerfully grow in knowledge of him.

The role of the Holy Spirit in our coming to this knowledge and in our prayer is all important. "These are the very things that God has revealed to us through the Spirit, for the Spirit reaches the depths of everything, even the depths of God" (1 Cor 2:10 JB). The Spirit from the depths of the Father reveals the Father to us; the Spirit in the depths of us prays to the Father. The final fruit of our listening to the word of God in Scripture and our responding in prayer is this twofold activity of the Holy Spirit—an activity which both conforms us to the image of Christ and brings about our union with the Father. The way of prayer is the way to the Father.

Part II

The Word of God

FIVE

The Word of God Comes in Human Words

In the beginning was the Word:
the Word was with God
and the Word was God.
He was with God in the beginning.
Through him all things came to be.

The Word became flesh
and made his dwelling among us,
and we have seen his glory:
the glory of an only son coming from the Father,
filled with enduring love.   John 1:1-3 JB, 14 NAB

IT IS SIGNIFICANT that the identity of one of the persons of the Trinity should be revealed as "the Word."

A word is something that is spoken. A word reaches out to communicate. A word is a bridge between people. When we speak, we not only convey information but we reveal something of ourselves. For a person of the Trinity to be "the Word" means that self-revelation is a part of the very nature of God.

Through the Word of God, the world was created. God spoke, and all things came into being. The Word of God is a word of power, a creative word, a word of love. Nothing compelled God to create the world but his love seeking expression.

We did not exist until God spoke in love. His love creates the one that he loves. When God says, "I love you," the "you" comes into being. We exist because God's word of love is spoken. We exist because when God speaks, the one who listens is created.

The all-powerful Word of God—the Word that brings the world into being—became flesh in Jesus of Nazareth. The Word of God was uttered as a man. John's Gospel does not say that the Word "entered into" flesh or "lived under the appearance" of flesh. John makes the blunt statement that the Word *became* flesh.

Nor is John content to say that the Word of God became man, or assumed human form. John deliberately states that the Word became *flesh*—a word carrying connotations of the weakness and temptation and mortality that is the lot of humankind. In Jesus of Nazareth, God did not play at becoming human, or walk the face of the earth disguised as a man. In Jesus Christ, the Word of God became a man, became flesh and bone, became one of us.

The Word of God became flesh, "and made his dwelling among us." A more literal translation of John's words would be "and pitched his tent among us." A note of familiarity strikes us: it is almost as if we would say, "The Word of God became a man, and moved in next door to us." He who created the world walked upon it. He whose love brought us into being lived with us as one of us.

It would be simpler for us to understand Jesus if he had been merely a very good man and not the Son of God. And, on the other hand, it would also be simpler to understand Jesus if he had not been truly human, if the Word of God had not completely become flesh. To reject the divinity of Jesus Christ, to reject that he is the Word of God, obviously runs contrary to the message of the gospel. But to reject his humanity, to reject that the Word *became flesh*, is no less a mistake. It is a mistake that we can unconsciously fall into, out of our reverence for Jesus Christ as the Son of God.

The Gospels give us many clues to the full humanity of Jesus, if we are but alert to them. We read of Jesus walking from Judea to Galilee, a distance of about sixty-five miles through very hilly country. He stopped at noon at the town of Shechem, "tired from his journey" (Jn 4:6 NAB) and thirsty, and asked a Samaritan woman for a drink of water. Do we *really* believe that he was tired and thirsty? We know that a long walk would exhaust us, and that we would indeed be very tired and thirsty by noontime. But do we accept that Jesus felt the same fatigue and aches that we do? Or do we unconsciously assume that he was some sort of first-century superman, gliding along a foot off the ground, never feeling the rocks of the road through his sandals?

The Word made flesh felt the same weariness and hunger and fatigue that we experience. He was "tempted in every way that we are" (Heb 4:15 NAB). Our faith in Jesus Christ, the Word of God, must take his full humanity into account. If we do not understand that the *Word became flesh*, we do not understand how God sent his Word to us.

In the same way, our listening to the word of God in Scripture must take the full humanity of that word into account. Jesus Christ is the Word of God become human. Scripture is the word of God in human words. If we only understand Scripture as the word of God, and not as the word of God spoken in human words, we will not be able to listen correctly to God speaking to us through Scripture. Conversely, if we only understand Scripture as words authored by human beings, and not as also the word of God, we will likewise fail to understand it.

How does God speak his word through the words of Scripture? How does God's word come to us in Scripture? We are tempted to believe that it is a word uttered from the heavens rather than a word uttered through human vocal cords. We are tempted to understand it as a disembodied word rather than a word made flesh.

Muslims believe that the Koran was dictated by the angel Gabriel to Mohammed. Mormons believe that their holy writings were found written in an unknown language upon tablets of gold. For a Christian, however, the words of God come not through angels but through human beings. They do not come in a mysterious language, but in human language. The words of God have been given to us in very human form, just as the Word of God is given to us become human.

We must respect how the word of God comes to us in order to listen to it correctly. We must accept its full humanness in order to have access to its divinity. Just as our faith is in the Word of God made flesh, so our approach to Scripture must be to the words of God taken fully human form.

THE WORD IN HISTORY

In order to understand the Bible properly we must understand its origin. God chose to have his word become flesh in the history of a specific people, a choice which gave his message a definite form. We will read Scripture with more understanding and listen to God's word speak to us more clearly the more we discover how Scripture was shaped and formed by the life of his chosen people. God chose the descendants of Abraham to be the vehicle of his voice; he chose that in the fullness of time his Son would be a descendant of Abraham. Our understanding of Scripture must begin with Abraham; our listening to the word of God must be as spiritual heirs of Abraham.

There is something mysterious, almost scandalous, about God's choice. It is a mystery why God should have picked out a specific individual some thirty-eight hundred years ago, asked him to leave his native land, and called him to be the father of a chosen people. Yet it is with Abram that God's revelation breaks into human history. Why this individual, and not another? Why, after centuries of darkness and silence, did God choose to speak at this time and not another? We cannot know. We can only know that this is how God has chosen to speak to humankind. We can only respect his choice, and listen to him as he has chosen to speak to us.

It is with Abram's journey to Canaan about 1850 B.C. that revelation begins. It is with Abram becoming Abraham, the father of faith, that men and women begin to rely upon God in faith and are changed by it. We too, even today, must become children of Abraham in order to listen to God in faith. What God speaks to us, he first began speaking to Abraham. The faith that we are called to live was first lived in an incomplete yet passionate way by Abraham. Abraham heard God speaking to him, and his life was changed.

Centuries later, the descendants of Abraham were a slave class in Egypt. It would be an exaggeration to call them a people; they were united by only the loosest of racial and religious ties. They preserved memories of their ancestors Abraham, Isaac, and Jacob, but professed only the sketchiest faith in the one true God. Around 1250 B.C., God selected Moses, a Sinai sheepherder who had grown up in Egypt, and revealed himself to him. God's word came unexpectedly from a burning bush, breaking into human history once again. God entrusted to Moses the mission of freeing the descendants of Abraham from their slavery in Egypt.

The origin of our Bible begins with the work and teaching of Moses. Our Scriptures have their roots in the writings and traditions that began crystalizing in the wake of Moses some three thousand years ago. Our Scriptures did not drop from heaven on tablets of gold; they were laboriously written and rewritten, line by line, over the course of a thousand years. If Abraham is the father of faith, Moses is the father of the Bible.

Moses was more than a great civil rights leader or powerful miracle worker. He was the instrument for forging the descendants of Abraham into a people. He took the weak ties of common ancestry and belief, and under the inspiration of God developed them into a common pattern of life and action. He not only led them out of Egypt; he led them into a pact together with God, that they should be God's people and God should be their God. He led them into a common consciousness and way of life.

We will not grasp the meaning of the Old Testament unless we understand that it is a book that grew out of the life of a people. If we divorce it from its origins, we will misunderstand it and misapply it in our own lives. This means that we must have some idea of what it means to be a people—a cultural experience most of us do not have.

In an era in which police departments and hospitals, social security and unemployment checks were unknown, a person's sheer survival depended upon belonging to a family, a tribe, a people. But a people held more in common than the means of physical survival. They had a common heritage, a common body of shared experiences. Our reminiscing at class reunions is but a very pale reflection of the collective memory of a people. When the people in question were the chosen people, then their heritage of memories centered on God's presence in their midst and the mighty deeds that he had performed for them in the past. As individuals we remember back to the days of our youth; as a people, they remembered back generations to the days of their origin.

We get to know another person both by what he or she says and does. The chosen people grew in their knowledge of God both through his words and through his actions. His revelation was contained as much in what happened to them as a people as in what he explicitly said to them. God initially revealed his nature to them more by events than by words. The words came later, as they began to understand the significance of the events.

Much of the Old Testament is taken up with writings that strike us as history. They are history, but a unique kind of history. The authors were more interested in the significance of the events than in the events themselves. Both dimensions are necessary for sacred history to be revelation. Unless an event occurred, there could be no significance. But without the significance, the event cannot function to reveal God's love for his people.

The Exodus of the Israelites out of Egypt was one of the most decisive events in the history of the chosen people. It was the event which constituted them as a people, which freed them from slavery, which started them on the road to becoming a kingdom, which set the pattern of life that they were to follow. It was an event in which later generations saw deep significance, and which has significance even for us.

The Exodus was an historical happening: something that

could be matter-of-factly reported on the evening news if it were to happen today. But the authors of the Old Testament were not content to merely report it, as a newscaster might. They told of it in such a way that its significance for them was brought out. They were much more concerned about its meaning for them than about its details.

The Old Testament began as the heritage of the chosen people, a heritage told from father to child. Each generation told the succeeding generation how they had come to be a people. "Do not forget the things your eyes have seen, nor let them slip from your heart all the days of your life; rather, tell them to your children and your children's children" (Dt 4:9 JB). They taught about God, and taught about what it meant to be a member of his chosen people, by recounting the events that marked their beginning. They taught about God's special concern for them by telling of the marvelous deeds he had done on their behalf. Recounting these events was more than an abstract history lesson: it was a preaching and teaching about God. "When your son asks you in days to come, 'What does this mean?' you will tell him, 'By sheer power Yahweh brought us out of Egypt, out of the house of slavery'" (Ex 13:14 JB).

In a culture where few can read, or afford to own anything written, teaching and preaching are part of a pattern of oral communication and collective memory. Ancient culture relied upon the spoken rather than the written word. Wisdom and traditions were passed from generation to generation by word of mouth rather than by books. When books were written, it was to preserve the oral heritage, not to replace it.

The very "handing-on" of oral tradition affects what is handed on. Stories tend to get remembered in set ways; a poetic form of expression will be adopted to make memorization easier. The constant telling and retelling of a story tends to round off the sharp edges, like the sea tossing and washing a small rock until it is round.

This influences the Bible we read today. Most of the Bible is a written expression of oral traditions, a writing down of a message that was first preached and taught and passed on from generation to generation by word of mouth. This oral handing-on has influenced the words we read and the form they are presented in.

God's words came to the chosen people not only through events which revealed God's presence and memories passed on from generation to generation. God's words were also spoken through the prophets, people who spoke in the name of God. The age of prophecy lasted from the time of David until after the exile. The golden age of prophecy came with Isaiah, Jeremiah, and Ezekiel, from around 750 to 500 B.C. These were the years in which Israel first teetered on the brink of conquest by foreign powers, then was invaded and carried off into exile, and finally permitted to return from exile. After about 400 B.C., prophecy died out and a famine came to Israel: "a famine not of bread, a drought not of water, but of hearing the word of God" (Am 8:11 JB).

Prophets spoke God's word to the chosen people. They spoke less of the future than of the present. They brought God's judgment to bear on the course that the chosen people were taking. Their message was often the same—a call to return to purity of faith in God—but each prophet addressed that message in terms of a specific historical situation and specific needs.

Old Testament prophecy must hence be read against the background of Old Testament history. Whether the chosen people were on the brink of conquest by foreign powers or whether they had been conquered and were in exile determined the specific word that God addressed to them through the prophets. The prophetic message before the exile was often a call to repentance, a warning that disaster would strike if they did not return to true worship of God. It was often uttered in uncompromising and even harsh terms. But God's prophetic word to the chosen people during their exile took on a different tone. It was a word of consolation and hope, a promise of deliverance.

When we read the prophetic books of the Old Testament, we need to keep in mind that they contain words addressed first of all to the chosen people at the time of the prophet and to the specific situation they were in. Ezekiel did not utter prophecies for twentieth-century Americans or Europeans; he proclaimed

God's word to sixth-century B.C. Israelites at the time of their exile into Babylon. Because God's word was truly spoken through Ezekiel, his prophecies contain God's revelation for all time. But it was a revelation addressed to people living over twenty-five hundred years ago, a word of God shaped by their situation and their needs. We are the indirect beneficiaries. Inspiration and meaning were in the first place bound up with the oral word addressed to specific listeners. We are privileged to "eavesdrop" on that conversation and through it hear the word of God addressed to us also.

In the Old Testament, both history and prophecy were seen as a manifestation of God's word. History was charged with meaning, charged with the revelation of God to his people. Prophecy was rooted in history: occurring within a historical context, bringing to light the significance in God's eyes of that moment in history, and tying together past, present, and future as the plan of God. The history was the history of a people; prophecy was God's word addressed to a people. The people of God were the context for the word of God to be spoken.

THE WORD BECOMES WORDS

God's activity in history cannot be limited to the inspiration of the writers of the Bible. The Holy Spirit guided and inspired not only the writers of the Bible, but also the prophets, judges, miracle workers, and leaders of the Old Testament, and the apostles, prophets, evangelists, teachers, and miracle workers of the New Testament.

In fact, while Scripture often describes the Holy Spirit guiding the leaders of the chosen people and the apostles in the early Church (Nm 11:16-25 and Acts 15:22-29, for example), and while it frequently speaks of the Spirit moving prophets to speak (2 Chr 24:20 and Acts 11:28, for example), it rarely if ever describes the Holy Spirit moving or inspiring writers to write the pages of Scripture. This does not mean that the Holy Spirit did not guide the writers of Scripture (for he did), but that this inspiration must be seen within the context of the Spirit's guidance of the chosen people and the Church. Within this context God guided the evolution of a body of literature that expressed the heritage of his people and his presence in their midst. Apart from this context, the writing of Scripture cannot be understood.

We should not imagine that God's voice came to the writers of Scripture in an audible way, giving them the exact words that they were to set down in writing. A voice from the heavens would have made more use of human ears than human understanding and receptivity to insight. Rather, the Spirit worked by inspiration—by giving insights, by endowing human beings with wisdom, by enabling them to understand the significance of God's presence to his people, by prompting them to write.

When Paul wrote his letters, Paul knew that he himself was writing the letters. He probably did not feel any different when he wrote the letters that later were included in the New Testament than he did in writing the letters which have been lost and are not a part of Scripture. Paul undoubtedly prayed for God's guidance and inspiration when he wrote, because he was writing to answer real needs of the early Church and wanted to answer those needs correctly. He sometimes stated that he was only giving his own opinions in his letters: "As for the other matters, although I know of nothing the Lord has said, I say... " (1 Cor 7:12 NAB). "About remaining celibate, I have no direction from the Lord but give my own opinion as one who, by the Lord's mercy, has stayed faithful" (1 Cor 7:25 NAB). Paul, then, was not attempting to write "Scripture," but to write the truth, to proclaim the gospel, to solve practical problems that were arising.

Nonetheless, Paul was inspired by the Holy Spirit, so that what he wrote could truly be accepted by the Church as a written part of the "new agreement" God was making with his people. God guided him when he wrote—but guided him without violating his freedom to write what he wanted to write. The Holy Spirit's guidance certainly did not prevent Paul's rather individual personality from showing through, and did not even prevent Paul from using a few expressions we might find impolite today (Gal 5:12, for example).

When we turn from books which had a single author (like an

epistle by Paul) to books which underwent a long process of development under several authors and editors (like Genesis), the matter of how the Holy Spirit's inspiration worked becomes even more complex. For us it is sufficient to know that the Spirit guided the evolution of each book and, indeed, of the entire body of literature that is the Bible.

Our modern concept of authorship is one of an author sitting down and writing a book. Many of the books of the Old Testament were not written in such a simple manner. Their "authorship" may have spanned centuries and involved many individuals in different ways. At the core of a book would have been an ancient tradition, faithfully handed down from generation to generation by word of mouth. Perhaps several slightly different oral traditions stemming from the same event were handed down in different geographic areas. In the continual telling and retelling of the event, the traditions took on a definite form.

At various points, each of the traditions was written down. The "authors" would not view their writing down of the tradition as a chance to be original and creative, but would view their task as being simply to preserve the tradition in writing as faithfully as they could. Their own insights and personalities, however, inevitably influenced their choice of traditions to preserve and words to capture them in.

At a later point in time—perhaps even centuries later—someone took on the work of "editing" the various written traditions into one work. Out of reverence for the material they were working with, the editors might choose to include several slightly different traditions without rewriting them to make them agree in details.

Years later a second, perhaps a third editor would set their hands to the book, incorporating other bits of written and oral tradition, working the book into the form in which we know it today. This "extended authorship" might go against our inclination of "one book, one author." But it is a very natural process when the book in question captures the religious heritage of a people and was told, written, and edited within the context of God's continuing presence to his people.

If we try to read the books of the Old Testament as if they all came from the hand of one author, we will become enmeshed in endless difficulties. If we attribute authorship directly to God himself, we will have to contend with his seeming inconsistencies and lapses of style. If we even view every book as each having its own author, difficult questions will arise. But if we view the Old Testament as the written religious heritage of a people, as the written result of God's continuing presence to them, then many problems do not arise and many questions become answerable.

Thus, the accounts in Exodus of the crossing of the Red Sea differ in details, but agree in the essential event and its significance: God acted to free his chosen people from slavery in Egypt by enabling them to cross the sea as if on dry land. One account has an east wind drying up the waters (Ex 14:21); another tradition has the waters pushed up as walls on each side (Ex 14:22). While the two traditions are not strictly compatible in detail, they agree in seeing the significance of the event: God enabled the Israelites to escape from Egypt through the sea.

There are two pitfalls we must avoid: on the one hand, not acknowledging that the Bible is the inspired word of God; on the other hand, believing that the Bible dropped down from heaven without the help of human hands or with only the unthinking secretarial services of the human authors. Both dangers are very real, and can effectively prevent God from speaking to us through the words of Scripture.

If we ignore the fact that the Bible is God's inspired, authoritative word to us, we will read it out of casual interest perhaps, but we will not read it as God's word to us. We may even seriously study it as an ancient text worthy of study, but we will not hear God speak to us through it, and our lives will not be changed by it.

If we do not acknowledge that the word of God was uttered in words of human beings, we will not be able to listen to God's word correctly. We will read the Bible as if it were a little voice whispering in our ear, reciting Genesis 1:1 to Revelation 22:21 in a monotone. Instead we must hear God's voice speaking through a symphony of human voices—voices which sometimes debate with each other, voices which sometimes speak in poetic form, sometimes in song. To confuse these voices is to confuse God's voice and to confuse ourselves.

In chapter two, the example of reading a magazine was given. We know that there are different types of writing in a magazine. We know that an editorial is not necessarily an objective statement of fact. We know that a short story is different from an article and has a different purpose. We know that a poem contains a different kind of truth than a cooking recipe.

We must bring the same kind of discernment to the pages of Scripture. We must accept that if God has chosen to speak to us in human language (as he has), then he can choose any form of human expression and writing to convey his message. He can reveal himself through poetry as well as prose, through fiction as well as history. Just as Jesus was not half human and half God, but fully human and fully divine, so the words of Scripture are not half human and half divine, but fully human and fully divine. They are truly the inspired words of God, his revelation of himself to us, but they are a revelation accomplished through the inspired efforts of human authors—writers who used many different literary forms and styles to express God's word.

The Bible is not a book but a library of books, written over a period of about one thousand years. Each book has its own personality and point of view; different books have quite different literary forms or ways of expressing truth. If we mistake one literary form for another, we mistake how God wishes to speak to us through that form, and what he wishes to say to us through it.

We cannot and do not demand that the parables of Jesus refer to actual historical events. Undoubtedly there were many sowers of seed, givers of wedding feasts, and landowners who let their vineyards out to tenants in the days of Jesus. That he had particular sowers or marriages or vineyards in mind is doubtful; he told the parables only to convey a truth that he wanted to teach. The apostles often asked about the meaning of the parables; it is never recorded that they asked the name of the sower, the date of the wedding feast, or the address of the vineyard.

In a similar way, some of the books of the Old Testament were written for the message they convey, without strict regard for facts of historicity or geography. The Book of Esther deals with Mordecai, who is represented as having been deported from Jerusalem by Nebuchadnezzar, but serving as an advisor to Ahasuerus—who ruled over one hundred years after Nebuchadnezzar died. The Book of Daniel takes similar liberties with dates and historical figures in conveying its message. This does not mean that these books are not inspired; it does mean that they are not attempting to teach history as such, but rather to teach us God's loving care for his people.

On the other hand, just as it is a mistake to demand that parables contain historically accurate information, so it is a mistake to dismiss the truly historical books of the Bible as if they were parables. The writers of biblical history were as interested in the significance of events as they were in the events themselves. But unless the events really did occur, there could be no significance seen in them. Unless God really did act to free the Israelites from Egypt and form a covenant with them, the chosen people would not have come into existence. Unless Jesus Christ really did live and teach, die on the cross and rise from the dead, any proclamation that he is Lord and Savior would be in vain.

When some of us hear for the first time that portions of the Bible were not necessarily written to record historical facts, we too quickly jump to the assumption that none of the Bible is historically reliable. In point of fact, however, archaeologists and Scripture scholars are finding ever increasing evidence of the trustworthiness of those portions of the Bible that were written to preserve historical accounts. John's "pool with five porticos" (Jn 5:2) has been discovered and excavated in Jerusalem. Research into ancient Mesopotamian laws has discovered that many incidents of Abraham's life described by Genesis are consistent with the culture in which he grew up.

To read Scripture as the word of God, we must read with understanding and discernment. We must have some understanding of the type of literature that each book of the Bible is and the intent of the author in writing it. We must neither demand that every book of the Bible conform to our modern ideas of historical accuracy, nor dismiss the whole Bible as a religious fairy tale. We must learn to read the opening chapters of Genesis differently than we read the four Gospels; to read Jonah differently than we read Kings; to read Revelation differently than we read Romans.

Reading each book of the Bible (and each section of each book) as the type of literature that it is allows us to focus on what the book does intend to teach. Our focus must be on what the author did intend to convey—which is the message that the Holy Spirit inspired and that the Lord wishes us to understand. In this way we will be able to listen to the word of God speak clearly to us through the words and types of literature in Scripture, his voice rising from the chorus of voices.

OUR BIBLE COMES TO BE

If we were to see the Book of Isaiah read by Jesus in the synagogue, or the actual letters Paul sent to Corinth, they would strike us as decidedly odd, even apart from their being in another language. Isaiah would have been preserved on a long scroll; the Hebrew alphabet it was written in contained no vowels. Paul's letters were written in Greek, but written all in capital letters, with words run together without spacing or punctuation.

Copies of the Scriptures were comparatively rare in Old Testament times and even in the time of Jesus. Few people could read or write; few owned "books." Writing was done on animal skins or on papyrus, a less expensive substance made from plants. But even a single sheet of papyrus cost perhaps a day's wages for the average worker. Sheets of papyrus were attached together to form a scroll. A scroll long enough to contain an Old Testament book could cost several months' wages. Obviously, the ordinary person could not afford to own the Scriptures with the same ease we can. Hence the importance of listening to the Scriptures read in the synagogue; hence the very early Church tradition of reading the Scriptures when Christians came together to worship and celebrate the Lord's Supper.

It is sobering to realize that parts of the Bible are about three thousand years old. We no longer have the original manuscripts that the authors made by hand or dictated. The oldest surviving editions of the New Testament date from about the fourth century, although many older manuscripts of individual books or fragments have been found. Different manuscripts sometimes read slightly differently or omit sections that other manuscripts include. The work of making a modern translation thus often includes the burden of deciding which ancient manuscript to follow.

The Bible first existed in the form of a collection of separate scrolls. We think of the Bible as a book; in the early part of its history, however, it was not a book but a number of books. Only gradually did the various books which make up the Bible come to be collected together and to be considered one book. And nowhere in the Bible is it stated which books make up the Bible. This is a decision which was inspired by God, to be sure, but a decision made by the Church under the guidance of the Holy Spirit.

At the time of Christ, two different editions of the books of the Old Testament were used by the Jewish people. Jews living in Palestine read their Scriptures in Hebrew, the language that they had spoken up to the time of the exile. (At the time of Jesus they spoke Aramaic, a closely related language.) Jews living in other parts of the world used a Greek translation of the Old Testament, since Greek was the common language where they lived. No definite listing of the books that did or did not belong to the Old Testament existed for the Jews until after the time of Christ, although there was agreement on the core of the Old Testament. The Greek edition of their Scriptures contained several books that the Hebrew edition did not contain.

When the Christian Church began, it generally used the Greek edition of the Old Testament, since it rapidly became a Gentile Christian Church and Greek was the most common language. The books we know as the New Testament were written in Greek—even Paul's letter to Latin-speaking Rome! When the New Testament writers wanted to quote the Old Testament, they naturally usually quoted it from the Greek edition of the Old Testament.

Although there was some discussion, the Church accepted the books contained in the Greek edition of the Old Testament as the books of the Old Testament until the time of the Protestant Reformation. At that time, the reformers termed those books which were in the Greek Old Testament but not in the Hebrew edition of the Old Testament as "apocryphal"—not to be treated as God's word on the same level as the accepted books of the Old Testament. The Council of Trent reaffirmed the tradition that these books are inspired parts of the Old Testament, and they are so read by Catholics and Orthodox today.

The New Testament went through a similar time of evolution and selection. Well over one hundred books or writings appeared in the early Church, claiming to be gospels or letters or revelations written by the apostles and Paul. Out of these, those that authentically expressed the faith of the Church and provided a reliable guide for the Christian life had to be chosen. While there was amazing consensus over what was inspired and what was not, it still required the Church's discussion and decision to select the books we read today as the New Testament. More will be said about this process in chapter seven.

All of us live with many harmless misconceptions, sometimes holding them to be eternal truths. People in China do not eat chop suey, and chili con carne isn't Mexican: both were invented in the United States. The tradition of "trick or treat" on Halloween is of recent vintage: the slogan was invented in 1937 by a dime store to increase candy sales. Most of these misconceptions are entirely harmless. But misconceptions about the Bible can cause us to hear the word of God incorrectly.

The table of contents of the Bible does not indicate the order in which the books of the Bible were written. It may appear to, because Genesis deals with creation and comes first, and Revelation seems to deal with the end of the world and comes last. But the actual order in which the books of the Bible were written bears little resemblance to the order in which they appear in the Bible.

In particular, we might assume that in the New Testament the Gospels were written first, then the epistles, then the Book of Revelation. Actually, some of Paul's letters were written before any of the Gospels, and almost all of the epistles were written before the Gospel of John. Nor are Paul's letters presented in the order in which they were written. They are presented in roughly the order of their length, with the longest, Romans, first.

We unconsciously assume that the Scriptures were written in chapter and verse, that Paul wrote his letter to the Romans in sixteen chapters. We may even unconsciously assume that Jesus spoke in verses, which the evangelists simply recorded. However helpful the divisions into chapters and verses may be for locating passages, they are not a part of Scripture and were not a part of the Bible as it was written. The Bible was first divided into chapters in the early part of the thirteenth century by Stephen Langton; division into verses was introduced by a printer, Robert Estienne, in 1551. If we made a reference to "John 3:16" to a first-century Christian—or even a twelfth-century Christian— we would get a blank stare.

More importantly, the chapter and verse divisions do not necessarily reflect a logical division of the text of Scripture. It is handy to read "a chapter a day," but the thought being developed by Paul may begin in the middle of one chapter and end in the middle of the next. Our reading should be guided by the meaning found in Scripture and the natural units of thought we find there, not by divisions introduced later. We should not hold our present system of numbering verses and chapters to be a "sacred" part of sacred Scripture.

THE WORD OF GOD IN HUMAN WORDS

The very human origins of the Bible can be difficult for us to accept. We can be scandalized by it. Or we can understand the human dimension of Scripture as an expression of God's love for us, as evidence of the lengths to which he went to draw us to himself.

The Bible contains the word of God in human language. It does not contain disembodied words of God, set down in writing by a fiery finger. It is not even a transcript of words uttered in thunder from the clouds, faithfully set down in writing by one or another stenographer.

We unconsciously resist fully accepting this. It is much easier—and much more romantic—to believe that an audible voice dictated the words of Scripture to various people, who in turn set them down in writing. It is more difficult to accept that God chose to reveal himself to us today through thoughts and words which were authentically the thoughts and words of human beings like ourselves.

We can become as scandalized at the humanness of God's words as were the Jews at the humanness of his Word: "Meanwhile the Jews were complaining to each other about him, because he had said, 'I am the bread that came down from heaven.' 'Surely this is Jesus son of Joseph' they said. 'We know his father and mother. How can he now say, "I have come down from heaven?"'" (Jn 6:41-42 JB).

It is easy to accept manna that mysteriously appears overnight as "bread come down from heaven." It is more difficult to accept the claim of Jesus that he indeed is bread sent to us. And even this claim would have been easier to accept if Jesus had mysteriously appeared in our midst, full grown and of unknown origin. But Jesus came into our midst in a quite ordinary appearing way: "We know his father and mother." How can he claim to be the Word of God?

The scandal the Jews felt at the humanity of Jesus is like the scandal we feel at his word in Scripture. "How can this word be the word of God come down from heaven? We know the men who wrote it: Isaiah, John, Paul. How can the writings of these men be the word of God?"

If we do not accept that the words of the Bible were fully the words of human beings, we do not understand them properly as the word of God—just as we do not understand Jesus as the

Christ if we do not accept his full humanity. Jesus was not merely a man, and the words of the Bible are not merely human words. But God's word to us must be accepted as fully human, whether spoken in an incomplete way in the words of the Bible or spoken in a full way in the person of Jesus of Nazareth.

SIX

It Is God Who Speaks

In times past, God spoke in fragmentary and varied ways to our fathers through the prophets; in this, the final age, he has spoken to us through his Son, whom he has made the heir of all things and through whom he first created the universe. This Son is the reflection of the Father's glory, the exact representation of the Father's being, and he sustains all things by his powerful word.

Hebrews 1:1-3 NAB

BEGINNING WITH ABRAHAM, God revealed himself to the human race. His revelation came in varied and fragmentary ways—not because God wished to withhold himself from humankind, but because human beings had to grow in their ability to recognize the voice of God. All too often the words of the prophets fell on deaf ears. All too often God spoke, but humans did not understand; all too often God acted, but humans failed to notice.

The Old Testament is the record of the fragmentary and varied ways that God spoke to people before the time of Jesus. The voice of God comes through the human voices of the Old Testament: Moses, Isaiah, Jeremiah, the author of the Books of Kings, the authors of the Psalms. God's voice must be heard through the chorus of voices, each of them conveying some aspect of the truth about God.

The voices of the Old Testament sometimes debate with each other. The almost cynical wisdom of Ecclesiastes must be heard alongside the often prosaic advice of Proverbs. Be diligent in your work, Proverbs advises, and you will be happy. It's not so simple, rejoins Ecclesiastes; much of humanity's busyness is empty.

Deuteronomy's central teaching is that when Israel is faithful to the commands of God she will prosper; when she disobeys him, disaster will befall her. The Books of Kings interpret Israel's history in terms of this principle: political disasters befall the chosen people because they have not been faithful. The same principle is applied to individuals: the just person will prosper, the unjust person will fall. "The just man shall flourish like the palm trees," proclaims Psalm 92:13 (NAB).

But this was not always borne out in experience. Sometimes the unjust flourished at the expense of the just. Sometimes evil seemed to prevail. The Book of Job must be read as another voice exploring this mystery. Countering the simple notion that the just person always flourishes, the Book of Job concerns itself with the problem of unjustified suffering.

Other passages in the Old Testament question whether the Deuteronomist's principle always holds true: is every political downfall a sign of infidelity? Psalm 44 laments:

> You let us go to the slaughterhouse like sheep,
> you scatter us among the nations.
> All day long I brood on this disgrace,
> my face covered in shame.
> All this happened to us though we had not forgotten you,
> though we had not been disloyal to your covenant;
> though our steps had not left your path:
> yet you crushed us in the place where jackals live,
> and threw the shadow of death over us.
> Why do you hide your face,
> and forget we are wretched and exploited?
>
> Psalm 44:11, 15, 17-19, 24 JB

Through the centuries of God's revelation the chosen people were gradually able to hear his voice more clearly. They began to understand God's repeated assurances of mercy and realize that he was a God of love and compassion. Early traditions attributed to God a wrath that was visited upon children for the sins of fathers (Ex 34:7); later traditions taught that each person would be punished only for his or her own sins (Dt 7:9-10; Jer 31:30; Ez 33:12-20).

The early descendants of Abraham saw Yahweh as a warrior God leading them into battle. "He gives the nations their deserts, smashing their skulls, he heaps the wide world with corpses" (Ps 110:6 JB). They saw in God the vengefulness against their enemies that they themselves felt—a vengefulness common in the Near East at that time. They believed that God himself willed the death of enemy women and children, as in the campaign of Saul against the Amalekites (1 Sm 15). Psalm 137 could pray, "A blessing on him who takes and dashes your babies against the rock" (v. 9 JB). Only gradually did they come to a fuller understanding of the mercy of God.

The word of God to the chosen people was a word which gradually drew them to himself, teaching them the path of love. To us, the law "an eye for an eye, a tooth for a tooth" is a harsh law of revenge. But in Old Testament times it was a law limiting vengeance to the amount of injury suffered. In Genesis, Lamech boasted that "I killed a man for wounding me, a boy for striking me. Seven-fold vengeance is taken for Cain, but seventy-seven-fold for Lamech" (Gn 4:23-24 JB). The law of Moses limited retaliation: "If a man injures his neighbor, what he has done must be done to him: broken limb for broken limb, eye for eye, tooth for tooth. As the injury inflicted, so must be the injury suffered" (Lv 24:19-20 JB).

Jesus brought to completion the teaching of the Old Testament. He taught, "You have learnt how it was said: 'Eye for eye and tooth for tooth.' But I say this to you: offer the wicked man no resistance. On the contrary, if anyone hits you on the right cheek, offer him the other as well" (Mt 5:38-39 JB). Jesus taught, "You have learnt how it was said: You must love your neighbor and hate your enemy. But I say this to you: love your enemies and pray for those who persecute you; in this way you will be sons of your Father in heaven" (Mt 5:43-45 JB).

Jesus Christ came as the fullness of God's revelation to the human race. God had spoken in fragmentary and varied ways in the past; now he spoke his complete Word to humanity in Jesus. The chosen people had only glimpses of the plan of God; in Jesus Christ, the Word became flesh, the mystery of God's plan was revealed. Paul wrote that the message that he preached "was a mystery hidden for generations and centuries and has now been revealed" (Col 1:26 JB). "If you read my words, you will have some idea of the depths that I see in the mystery of Christ. This mystery that has now been revealed through the Spirit to his holy apostles and prophets was unknown to any in past generations" (Eph 3:4-5 JB).

Because of the revelation of God that we have in Jesus Christ, we can now read the Old Testament with a fuller understanding. We can read many passages in it as a foreshadowing of Jesus, even when these passages only offer a partial glimpse of God's plan to send us his Son. Early Christians read and understood the Old Testament in this way, and found enrichment for their spiritual lives.

Many of the Old Testament passages which foreshadow the coming of Jesus were not written simply for such a purpose. Psalm 2 was most likely composed to celebrate the coronation of a king of Israel; Psalm 22 could be spoken by any suffering person turning to God for help; Psalm 110 probably referred to the king ruling Israel at the time it was written. But if we read these psalms with Jesus in mind, we find in them glimpses of the mystery of Christ. All three are quoted by New Testament writers as prophetic references to Jesus.

Paul in his preaching applied the words of Psalm 2 to Jesus: "You are my son; today I have become your father" (Ps 2:7 and Acts 13:33 JB). Jesus himself prayed the words of Psalm 22 on the cross, giving this psalm a special reference to himself: "My God, my God, why have you deserted me?" (Ps 22:1 and Mt 27:46 JB). The opening words of Psalm 110—"The Lord said to my Lord, 'Sit at my right hand till I make your enemies your footstool'" (Ps 110:1 NAB)—are applied to Jesus Christ several times in the New Testament, once by Jesus himself in a discussion with the Pharisees (Mt 22:44). Peter quoted them to proclaim the Lordship of Jesus in his Pentecost sermon (Acts 2:34-35), and the letter to the Hebrews uses them to teach that Jesus is at the right hand of the Father (Heb 1:13; 8:1; 10:12-13).

Likewise, many passages from the prophets can be understood as references to Jesus—dim foreshadowings made clear by the light of his coming. We are able to understand the words of the prophets in a fuller sense than the first listeners were because we have received God's full revelation in Jesus Christ.

Our safest guide in applying Old Testament passages to Jesus is the New Testament. We should pay attention to the way the New Testament uses the passage from the Old Testament that it applies to Jesus. If the edition of the Bible that we are reading provides the Old Testament reference for such quotes, we can turn to the original Old Testament passages and read them with fuller understanding.

We should be cautious in giving any passage from Scripture a meaning beyond that intended by the author. Any fuller interpretation should always grow out of the meaning that the author did intend and be consistent with the rest of God's revelation. But we can profitably read and understand the Old Testament in the light of the New; we can understand the varied and fragmentary ways God revealed himself in the past in the light of the revelation made to us in Jesus Christ.

Jesus was more than the one who revealed the mystery of God's plan for humankind. He did more than complete the revelation of God begun in the Old Testament. Jesus Christ not only brought God's message to us; he was God's message. We cannot separate what he said from who he is if we are to hear his words as words of life.

THE WORD OF LIFE

Jesus proclaimed that "This is indeed the will of my Father, that all who see the Son and believe in him may have eternal life;

and I will raise them up on the last day" (Jn 6:40 NRSV). This bold claim caused many of his followers to leave him. It was easier for them to accept Jesus as a great leader than as the Son of God; it was easier to accept a promise of a better life here and now than a promise of eternal life.

But Jesus did not back away from his claim. He instead emphasized that the words he spoke were words that gave the life of the Spirit to those who listened to them: "It is the Spirit that gives life, the flesh has nothing to offer. The words I have spoken to you are spirit and they are life" (Jn 6:63 JB). Those who did not turn away from Jesus recognized the power and promise of his words. Peter confessed, "You have the message of eternal life" (Jn 6:68 JB).

The apostles were not invited merely to learn truths about God from the mouth of Jesus, but invited to know God himself. They were not merely asked by Jesus to preserve and pass on a set of truths; they were asked to become "servants of the Word," servants of Jesus Christ. Their mission was less to pass on information about God than to make the Word of God present in the midst of humanity. The book that resulted from their ministry, the New Testament, is less interested in teaching us facts about God than in instructing us how to enter into a relationship with him.

We can know a great many facts about someone but not really know him or her if we have never met that person. We can know their age, height, weight, occupation; but no matter how many of these facts are added up, we would still not know them if we had never seen them face-to-face. For the Hebrew, to "know" was to experience; to know someone was to be intimately united with them. Thus Genesis states that "Adam knew Eve his wife, and she conceived and bore Cain" (Gn 4:1 RSV). Paul speaks of Christ as one who "knew no sin" (2 Cor 5:21 RSV). Obviously Christ "knew" what sin was; Paul's meaning is that Christ was not guilty of (did not participate in) sin.

Thus when Jesus speaks of the Son knowing the Father and the Father knowing the Son (Mt 11:27), he is talking of the intimate union of the Father and the Son. And when Jesus in his prayer to the Father says that "eternal life is this: to know you, the only true God, and Jesus Christ whom you have sent" (Jn 17:3 JB), he is speaking of knowing the Father in the sense of being united with the Father. Eternal life comes from hearing the word of God and through it "knowing" God: entering into a relationship with him. The words of Jesus are words of life because they enable us to know the Father, to enter into the relationship with God by which we are his children.

The basic revelation that comes through Scripture is the revelation of God himself. The Bible is unlike any other book because through the inspiration of the Holy Spirit (inspiring its writing and inspiring our reading) we can hear words of eternal life, we can come to know God, we can enter into a relationship with God.

It is God who speaks to us through the Bible. He does not merely give us words about himself; his revelation to us is his Word become flesh. Jesus did not live among us merely to refine the moral code of the Old Testament; he came to make his Father known to us as our Father. The Holy Spirit does not merely guarantee the correctness of what the Bible says; the Holy Spirit comes to give us life.

For our part, we cannot approach Scripture as we would any other book. It is not a book of ancient facts; it is not even merely a record of God's past revelations. It is a means whereby God reveals himself today, a means whereby the word of life is addressed to us today. The word of God written in Scripture is not a dead word; it is a living word, a word that is addressed to us here and now, a word that brings us life today.

God's revelation that comes to us through the pages of Scripture is a revelation of himself. Our Father in heaven is a person, his revelation is the revealing of himself to us. For God to allow us to know him as he is, he had to do more than send us a book of facts. He had to do more than send us prophets who spoke in his name. In order for him to reveal himself to us, he had to send his Son to become one of us. And he had to send his Spirit to live in us, to give us the very life that Jesus Christ himself lived.

A basic belief of Christianity is that God has spoken to us and continues to speak to us. A basic belief of Christianity is that we do not have to search after God, but that God searches us out and reveals himself to us. A basic belief of Christianity is that Jesus was not merely a great prophet, speaking the words of God, but that Jesus of Nazareth is the Word of God.

Jesus was both the messenger and the message. Because of who he was, we can enter into relationship with God. His words, if we listen to them, bring us knowledge of God; his words bring us into relationship with God. His words are words of life; the inspiration of the Spirit in us is life itself.

Our reading of the Scripture must be reading in which we encounter the God who reveals himself through the words of Scripture. We must be attentive to what Jesus revealed about himself, what he told us about his Father, and what he promised to give us through the Holy Spirit. In order to read Scripture as the word of God, we must be filled with a desire to grow in union with God—Father, Son, and Holy Spirit.

ABBA

Psalm 103 proclaims, "As a father has compassion on his children, so the Lord has compassion on those who fear him" (v. 13 NAB). God spoke to the chosen people through Jeremiah the prophet, saying: "I thought you would call me, My Father, and would not turn from following me" (Jer 3:19 RSV). Yet the passages in the Old Testament which call God "Father" are few—only about fifteen in all.

By contrast, Jesus in the Gospels constantly uses the term "Father" for God, especially in his prayers. Jesus calls God "Father" about one hundred seventy times in the Gospels, most frequently in the Gospel of John. And whereas the Old Testament used the term almost exclusively for God as the Father of the whole chosen people, Jesus spoke of God as "*My* Father." Even more significantly, the Aramaic word Jesus used to refer to his Father was "abba"—which could be literally translated "dada" or "daddy." "'Abba (Father)!' he said, 'Everything is possible for you. Take this cup away from me. But let it be as you, not I, would have it'" (Mk 14:36 JB).

Addressing God as "Abba" would have been unthinkable to devout Jews at the time of Christ. Even to refer to God as "*My* Father" would have been considered presumptuous, but to address God with the familiar "abba" or "daddy" would have been considered presumptuous to the point of blasphemy. Yet Jesus did this—claiming such a familiar relationship with God that the informal and intimate term "abba" could be used. Jesus claimed that God was his Father and that the relationship between them was so close and loving that he could indeed call upon God as a child would his father.

This special relationship with God lay at the heart of Jesus' life and mission. He was the Son of God. All that he did, all that he taught, all that he accomplished had importance solely because he was the Son of God.

> I am the Way, the Truth and the Life.
> No one can come to the Father except through me.
> If you know me, you know my Father too.
> From this moment you know him and have seen him....
> To have seen me is to have seen the Father,
> so how can you say, "Let us see the Father"?
> Do you not believe
> that I am in the Father and the Father is in me?
> The words I say to you I do not speak as from myself:
> it is the Father, living in me, who is doing this work.
> You must believe me when I say
> that I am in the Father and the Father is in me.
>
> **John 14:6-7, 9-11 JB**

Jesus lived among us as the revelation of the Father. Because he was truly the Son of God—able to address God as Abba, Father—those who saw Jesus saw the Father. Jesus was not merely a messenger of God, a word spoken by God to human-kind, as through one of the Old Testament prophets. Jesus was in such a relationship to the Father that he himself was the message of God, the Word of God to us. The revelation made in Jesus was not a revelation about God, but a revelation of God himself.

Through Jesus God revealed himself as our Father. The parable of the prodigal son (Lk 15:11-32) is really the parable of the loving father, searching the horizon for the return of his lost son, forgiving him without quibble or question, welcoming him back with a party. Our Father in heaven is a Father whose love goes far beyond the love of human fathers: "If you, then, who are evil, know how to give your children what is good, how much more will your Father in heaven give good things to those who ask him!" (Mt 7:11 JB). He is a Father who knows our every need (Mt 6:32) and who has prepared an eternal home for us: "There is no need to be afraid, little flock, for it has pleased your Father to give you the kingdom" (Lk 12:32 JB).

Jesus spent much time in prayer, talking with his Father. Sometimes he spent the night in prayer (Lk 6:12); sometimes he openly acknowledged his close union with the Father through prayer (Jn 11:41). Being with the Father in prayer was an expression of his Sonship. "Once he was in a certain place praying, and when he had finished one of his disciples said, 'Lord, teach us to pray, just as John taught his disciples.' He said to them, 'Say this when you pray: "Father, may your name be held holy, your kingdom come..."'" (Lk 11:1-2 JB).

Jesus authorized his followers to address his Father just as he did. He lets us be so bold as to say to God, "Our Father...." Through Jesus Christ, we can enter into a relationship with God; we can become sons and daughters of the Father of Jesus. "I am ascending to my Father and your Father, to my God and your God" (Jn 20:17 JB). Through the Son of God, we can become sons and daughters of God, children of God. "It was then that, filled with joy by the Holy Spirit, he said, 'I bless you, Father, Lord of heaven, and of earth, for hiding these things from the learned and the clever and revealing them to mere children. Yes, Father, for that is what it pleased you to do. Everything has been entrusted to me by my Father; and no one knows who the Son is except the Father, and who the Father is except the Son and those to whom the Son chooses to reveal him'" (Lk 10:21-22 JB).

The kingdom of heaven is promised to those who call upon God as Abba, Father—to those who become as little children, entering into an intimate and loving relationship with God. "I tell you solemnly, anyone who does not welcome the kingdom of God like a little child will never enter it" (Mk 10:15 JB). The promise of heaven is based on our entering into a relationship: becoming a child of God, being adopted by the Father through Jesus Christ.

Jesus brought us the full revelation of who God is: he brought us the revelation that God is our Father. He was able to bring us that revelation precisely because God was his Father. What he brought us was less a fact than an opportunity; he was less interested in teaching us about the nature of God than in enabling us to enter into a relationship with God, such that we can call upon him as "Abba, Father." Through Jesus, we both see the Father and have access to him.

THE WAY, THE TRUTH, THE LIFE

Jesus' claim was very bold: "I am the Way, the Truth and the Life. No one can come to the Father except through me. To have seen me is to have seen the Father" (Jn 14:6, 9 JB). What is the Way of Jesus? What is the Truth of his claim that to have seen him is to have seen the Father? What is the Life that he promises us? If our reading of Scripture is to get beyond the surface of the words, these questions are ones we must reflect upon.

The way: "Follow me." Jesus' invitation to his disciples was quite simple: "Follow me." For men and women to come to know the Father and to become his sons and daughters, they had to accept Jesus. The way to the Father is the way of Jesus. The call that Jesus addresses to us today is the same call: "Follow me."

Following Jesus requires more than calling oneself a Christian, or being a passive member of a church, or learning a lot about Christianity, or obeying a moral code. Following Jesus involves entering into a personal relationship with him, acknowledging him as our Lord and Savior. We are not invited to be respectful spectators of Jesus' life from a distance; Jesus invites us to walk alongside him and to obey him.

To follow Jesus involves more than taking one step on the path that he laid out. It means following after him, day after day. It means constantly renewing our commitment to him. And it means modeling our lives on his. Jesus invites us, not merely to tag along after him, but to imitate him, to grow up into his image. To accept the call to follow Jesus means to make him the focus of our lives, the image constantly before our eyes. He must become our way of life.

The way to the Father is the way of Jesus Christ of Nazareth. "There is no salvation through anyone else, nor is there any other name under heaven given to the human race by which we are to be saved" (Acts 4:12 NAB). Hence it is that we must turn to Jesus Christ and accept him as Lord in order to have forgiveness of our sins and receive life. Hence it is that his call, "Follow me," assumes such seriousness when we hear it. Jesus Christ was not merely a great prophet arisen among us; he is the Word of God to us, the access to the Father provided for us. He is the Way.

The truth: "To see me is to see the Father." When people saw Jesus, what did they see? The appearance of Jesus was certainly not otherworldly. However he appeared to Peter, James, and John during his transfiguration on the mountain, he must have normally looked like an ordinary human being. His neighbors in Nazareth apparently saw nothing extraordinary about him. Considering him to be only a carpenter's son turned preacher, they failed to have faith in him. Even his relatives were baffled that people would gather in crowds to listen to him: "He went home again, and once more such a crowd collected that they could not even have a meal. When his relatives heard of this, they set out to take charge of him, convinced he was out of his mind" (Mk 3:20-21 JB). If his appearance had been in any way extraordinary, no doubt greater reverence would have been shown to him.

Even after his resurrection from the dead, Jesus did not appear to people in a dazzling light. Mary Magdalene mistook the risen Christ for the gardener (Jn 20:15)—something that would have been unthinkable if Jesus' appearance was in any way to go beyond mere physical appearance: Jesus looked like an ordinary human being.

The clue to seeing the Father in Jesus was provided by Jesus himself: "You must believe me when I say that I am in the Father and the Father is in me; believe it on the evidence of this work, if for no other reason" (Jn 14:11 JB). The works that Jesus did are the clue to seeing the Father. When John the Baptist sent some of his followers to Jesus to ask whether he was the messiah who had been promised, Jesus gave this response: "Go back and tell John what you hear and see; the blind see again, the lame walk, lepers are cleansed, and the deaf hear, and the dead are raised to life and the Good News is proclaimed to the poor; and happy is the man who does not lose faith in me" (Mt 11:4-6 JB).

The works that Jesus did were not mere signs and wonders— a magic show demonstrating his superhuman power. They had a deeper significance: they were an assault on the kingdom of darkness to repair the sickness and death that afflict the world because of sin. They were works of love, works revealing the Father's love for humankind. Just as we are concerned when our children are sick or hungry, so our heavenly Father is concerned for us. This concern was expressed in Jesus by his works, works which revealed the Father's love for humanity.

The life: "Love as I have loved you." Jesus' works carried a special meaning for his followers. They were not merely signs of God's love to be admired; they were not merely occasions for thanking God for his love for us. They were works to be performed by the followers of Jesus in imitation of him. "Believe me that I am in the Father and the Father is in me, or else believe because of the works themselves. Amen, amen, I say to you, whoever believes in me will do the works that I do, and will do greater ones than these, because I am going to the Father" (Jn 14:11-12 NAB).

The works that we are to do in imitation of Jesus are not primarily extraordinary miracles, but the works of love. "I give you a new commandment: Love one another. Such as my love has been for you, so must your love be for each other. This is how all will know you for my disciples: your love for one another" (Jn 13:34-35 NAB). This new command might not seem revolutionary to us, but when Jesus first proclaimed it, it must have struck his disciples as new indeed.

The Old Testament Law read, "You shall love your neighbor as yourself" (Lv 19:18 NAB). And whenever the law of love came up during Christ's ministry he merely reaffirmed this Old Testament Law (Mt 19:16ff; 22:34ff; Lk 10:25ff). But during the intimacy of the Last Supper, Jesus revealed a new law for his disciples to follow: not merely love of others according to the standard by which we love ourselves, but love of others according to the standard set by Jesus.

Jesus also demonstrated the meaning of the new command by washing the disciples' feet during the Last Supper. This was a lowly service usually performed by a household slave, and Peter rebelled at the idea of his Lord doing it. But Jesus deliberately washed their feet and then told the disciples, "What I just did was to give you an example: as I have done, so you must do" (Jn 13:15 NAB). His love was a love of humble service—a love that went far beyond merely extending self-love to others. It was a radically self-sacrificing love.

Jesus' love for his apostles was love to the point of death. That realization must have come to the apostles during the Last Supper, for they knew that this was to be literally their last supper together before Jesus died. Jesus had told them that his hour had come, that he was returning to the Father and glorification—but returning by way of Calvary, for their sakes. This too was a part of the new command: "This is my commandment: love one another as I have loved you. There is no greater love than this: to lay down one's life for one's friends" (Jn 15:12-13

NAB). Jesus could not have made the meaning of his new commandment any clearer to his apostles than by presenting it to them on the eve of his death. "Such as my love has been for you, so must your love be for each other" (Jn 13:34 NAB).

In Jesus we see the Father; in the love that Jesus has for us, we see the love that his Father and our Father has for us. In following Jesus we have our way to the Father. In listening to the words of Jesus and obeying them, we enter into union with the Father: "Those who love me will keep my word, and my Father will love them, and we will come to them and make our home with them" (Jn 14:23 NRSV). In Jesus, we have life.

Although Jesus does not physically walk in our midst today, he is still with us, he is still our life. Through him we can be in union with God: "In a short time the world will no longer see me; but you will see me, because I live and you will live. On that day you will understand that I am in my Father and you in me and I in you" (Jn 14:19-20 JB).

As the Way, the Truth, the Life, Jesus is the revelation of God come to the world. He gives us not merely knowledge about God, but knowledge of God; not merely a message from a distant God, but a path to our Father; not merely a description of the good life, but life itself. And he gives us all this through his Holy Spirit.

THE SPIRIT OF GOD

In all four Gospels, John the Baptist introduces Jesus by announcing that through him salvation will come to the world, and in all four Gospels, John proclaims Jesus as the one who will enable men and women to live by the Holy Spirit: "I have baptized you with water, but he will baptize you with the Holy Spirit" (Mk 1:8 JB). Jesus himself promised that he would send the Spirit—as living waters for the thirsty (Jn 7:37-38), as one who would lead us into the truth (Jn 14:26; 16:13), as the power of God present in our lives (Lk 24:49; Acts 1:5, 8). The life that Jesus brings is the life of the Spirit.

The Holy Spirit was sent on Pentecost day, and the Church sprang to life. Where before the apostles had been fearful and uncertain, with the power of the Spirit they were bold in proclaiming Jesus Christ as the Savior of the world.

But the presence of the Spirit in our lives is more than simply a matter of power and boldness. The Spirit is first of all the Spirit of adoption: "For those who are led by the Spirit of God are children of God. For you did not receive a spirit of slavery to fall back into fear, but you received a spirit of adoption, through which we cry, 'Abba, Father!' The Spirit itself bears witness with our spirit that we are children of God" (Rom 8:14-16 NAB). Jesus taught us about our heavenly Father; the Holy Spirit living in us lets us address God as "Abba, Father" just as Jesus himself did. "As proof that you are children, God sent the spirit of his Son into our hearts, crying out, 'Abba, Father!'" (Gal 4:6 NAB). It is through the Holy Spirit living in us that we are authorized to call upon God as our Father.

The Holy Spirit is the Spirit of Christ, the Spirit that guided him through his life and ministry. The same Holy Spirit lives in us to conform us to the image of Christ, to guide us in following the footsteps of Christ.

The earmarks of the presence of the Spirit in our lives—love, joy, peace, patience, kindness, goodness, trustfulness, gentleness, self-control (Gal 5:22)—were all characteristics of the life of Jesus. We have the power to sacrifice ourselves in love, just as Christ sacrificed himself in love, through the Holy Spirit. We receive true joy from the Holy Spirit, just as Jesus did: "It was then that, filled with *joy* by the Holy Spirit, he said..." (Lk 10:21 JB). The peace of Jesus that he promised to us is the peace that results from the Spirit reigning in our lives: "Peace I bequeath to you, my own peace I give you, a peace the world cannot give, this is my gift to you" (Jn 14:27 JB).

Paul wrote that the greatest gift of the Holy Spirit is the gift of love (1 Cor 13:13). We must understand that gift in terms of the new command of Jesus: to love as he loved. Such a love to the point of self-sacrificing death is beyond our own capability. We need the power of the Spirit to love as Jesus loved. And indeed, the power of the Spirit is the power to love with the same love that Jesus loved: the love of the Father for us. God so loved the world that he sent his Son to us. God so loves the world now that he gives us the power to love with his love, to love with the love of Christ, through the Spirit of Christ living in us.

There are different ways to express the central truth of Christianity. We can say that to be a Christian is to be adopted as sons and daughters of God. We can say that to be a Christian is to be filled with the Holy Spirit. We can say that to be a Christian is to be in Christ, to put on Christ. We can say that to be a Christian is to be a member of the body of Christ. We can say that it is to accept Christ as our Savior and be reconciled to God by his death and resurrection.

All of these statements speak of the same mystery and capture aspects of it. We can attempt to express what it means to be a Christian in terms of our relationship to the Father, or to Jesus Christ, or to the Holy Spirit. But although there are three persons in God, there is one God and one mystery of him drawing us to himself. Paul expressed this mystery in these words:

> The Spirit of God has made his home in you. In fact, unless you possessed the Spirit of Christ you would not belong to him. Though your body may be dead it is because of sin, but if Christ is in you then your spirit is life itself because you have been justified; and if the Spirit of him who raised Jesus from the dead is living in you, then he who raised Jesus from the dead will give life to your own mortal bodies through his Spirit living in you. **Romans 8:9-11 JB**

Our reading of Scripture takes place within the context of this action of God to give us life and draw us to himself. What ultimately makes the words of Scripture unlike any other words is the reality behind them: the plan of the Father to adopt us as his children through Jesus Christ, giving us the life of the Holy Spirit. Reading Scripture as the word of God cannot be divorced from participating in this plan of salvation.

Hence the role of the Holy Spirit in our reading is more than a matter of his giving understanding to our minds and touching our hearts. The Holy Spirit is more than a study guide, and his role is to do more than simply make us feel good when we read the Bible. His role is most basically to give us life—God's life. Our reading of Scripture is an occasion of our growing in that life.

The Holy Spirit inspires our reading in order that he may literally inspire life into us, that he may be the breath of God breathed into us to give life to us. To "inspire" is literally to "breathe in." One of the authors of Genesis conceived of the first creation of humanity in this way: "Yahweh God fashioned man of dust from the soil. Then he breathed into his nostrils a breath of life, and thus man became a living being" (Gn 2:7 JB). John's Gospel tells us that after Jesus' resurrection he sent his apostles out to carry on his mission, and "after saying this he breathed on them and said, 'Receive the Holy Spirit'" (Jn 20:22 JB). The inspiration of the Holy Spirit in us is more than a matter of giving insight to our understanding; his inspiration is a breath of life. The word of God to us is a word of life.

It is God himself who speaks to us through the pages of Scripture, revealing himself to us. We are given the Holy Spirit not only so that we can understand God's revelation, but so that we may live the divine life. Jesus came not merely to teach us facts about God, but to give us a way to come to the Father.

The plan of Jesus included much more than leaving behind an inspired book; Jesus came so that we might receive the Holy Spirit and be an inspired people, a Spirit-filled people. The plan of Jesus was to create a Church in which his Spirit would live and through which people would come to know God's love for them. It is God who speaks to us through the words of Scripture; it is, above all, the Church that hears this word of life.

SEVEN

It Is the Church Who Listens

Those who accepted his message were baptized, and about three thousand persons were added that day. They devoted themselves to the teaching of the apostles and to the communal life, to the breaking of the bread and to the prayers. Awe came upon everyone and many wonders and signs were done through the apostles. All who believed were together and had all things in common; they would sell their property and possessions and divide them among all according to each one's need. Every day they devoted themselves to meeting together in the temple area and to breaking bread in their homes. They ate their meals with exultation and sincerity of heart, praising God and enjoying favor with all the people. And every day the Lord added to their number those who were being saved. Acts 2:41-47 NAB

PENTECOST WAS THE TURNING POINT for Christianity. After Christ ascended into heaven, his followers huddled together in the upper room, not certain what to do, waiting for the coming of the Holy Spirit that had been promised. They were few in number: about one hundred twenty, including the eleven that Jesus had commissioned as apostles.

If their past performance was any indication, not too much could be expected from the followers Jesus left behind. With few exceptions, they had all deserted Jesus in his hour of need, during his trial and death. Even after his resurrection they had been fearful and slow to believe. Up to the very time of his ascension, they had still been looking for Jesus to establish an earthly empire and restore the kingdom of David to Israel.

Pentecost transformed this unpromising group of people into the core of the Church. The coming of the Holy Spirit gave them the power to boldly proclaim what they knew about Jesus Christ, what they had seen and heard. The inspiration of the Holy Spirit gave them the insight to finally understand the fulfillment of the Old Testament prophecies in Jesus Christ.

In Luke's presentation of the events in Acts, the early Church seems to spring forth full grown on Pentecost day. In the aftermath of the coming of the Holy Spirit, the followers of Christ band together for prayers and for the basic pattern of their lives. People who must have been strangers before, people of different languages even, begin living together, sharing their possessions with each other, finding the focus of their lives in what they have in common in Jesus Christ.

After Pentecost day, the context of the New Testament is the early Church. There are great personalities who capture our attention, particularly Paul and his missions. But Paul worked to lay the groundwork for the spread of the Church. Luke singled out Paul in the last half of the Book of Acts in order to demonstrate the spread of the gospel and the Church "even to the ends of the earth." It is no accident that Paul did not volunteer for his first missionary journey: the Church in Antioch, acting under the inspiration of the Holy Spirit, selected him and sent him out.

Today we may take the Church so much for granted that we do not realize its full importance. We may be tempted to think that membership in the Church is something separate from belief in Jesus Christ—a "fringe benefit." Or we may conceive of membership in the Church as a part-time concern, something that is not at the center of our lives. Either attitude would have been unthinkable in the early Church.

Peter's sermon on Pentecost day was a proclamation of the Lordship of Jesus Christ. When people's hearts were touched and they asked him, "What must we do?" Peter replied, "You must repent and every one of you must be baptized in the name of Jesus Christ for the forgiveness of your sins, and you will receive the gift of the Holy Spirit" (Acts 2:37-38 JB). Peter did not say, "You must join the Church." Peter simply said, "Repent, be baptized in Christ, receive the Holy Spirit." But the *result* of men and women repenting, being baptized, and receiving the Holy Spirit was the creation of the Church: "That very day about three thousand were added to their number...." The *result* of Peter's proclamation was the creation of a fellowship, centered on prayer and nourished by the teaching of the apostles. There is certainly no grounds in Acts for divorcing belief in Jesus Christ from membership in his Church.

Nor was membership in the early Church a limited commitment, a duty to be discharged by worshipping together once a week. Membership in the early Church was a matter of one's whole life being joined with other Christians. The things that people held dearest—possessions and time—were put in common. While not every early Church community followed the same pattern of common ownership as the Jerusalem community, it is clear that joining the early Church meant a rather complete reorganization of one's life. One couldn't be a member of the Church on a part-time basis.

When we compare the state of things before and after Pentecost day, it is clear that the Holy Spirit played an indispensable role. Without the power and guidance of the Holy Spirit, the apostles would likely have died of old age in the upper room. With the Holy Spirit, thousands were drawn to faith in Jesus Christ and drawn to completely reorganize their lives so that Jesus Christ became their focus.

In order to more fully understand this, we need to reflect on how Christ carried out his mission during his public ministry. And this in turn will provide us with the key to understanding the place of Scripture in the Church.

THE PLAN OF JESUS

If we were to read the Gospels as if for the first time, without any preconceived ideas, we would be struck by how unlikely an approach Jesus took to saving the world. Jesus did none of the things that we would do if we set out to change the course of history.

Rome was the political center of the Western world at the time of Jesus; if we had wanted to influence the world, we would have chosen Rome for our starting point. God did not. Instead, he chose to send his Son as a Jew, a member of an inconsequential people without political power. They had had their peak of power under David and Solomon; after that their kingdom had steadily slid into disrepair, finally ending in the disaster of the exile. For centuries before Christ, Jews had been a subject people, periodically rebelling to regain their independence, but never with lasting success. At the time of Christ, they were an insignificant part of the Roman empire, with no political hope.

If we were to forego political means for influencing history, we would next choose the influence of ideas. But Jerusalem was not the intellectual center of the world; the chosen people had never been the cultural leaders of their times. In the realm of philosophy, no ancient civilization matched Greece in the time of Socrates, Plato, and Aristotle. Yet Jesus was not born a Greek, a disciple of Aristotle. He was born a Jew.

If we could not influence the political or cultural trends of our time, we would at least try to attract a large following for ourselves. Here again the focus of Jesus was different. While Jesus did preach to the multitudes, he spent most of his time with a small number of apostles and disciples. Most of his effort went into preparing a small band of followers to carry on his mission. His emphasis was not on numbers: he resisted the attempts of the crowds to crown him king, and he never watered down his hard sayings to keep the allegiance of half-hearted followers.

The strategy that Jesus followed was to select a small number of rather ordinary people, ask them to wholeheartedly dedicate their lives to him, and train them to carry out his mission. His basic training program was to invite them to live with him. When he invited someone to follow him, his words meant literally that: to follow him as he walked the countryside of Judea and Galilee.

Jesus' selection of followers was also curious. He did not choose the religious leaders of his time. He did not even choose educated people, for the most part. His band of followers was made up of very ordinary people—fishermen, housewives, civil service clerks. As we see them described in the Gospels, none of them strike us as very likely candidates for undertaking great responsibilities.

But it was this group of people that received most of Jesus' time and attention. He taught them, he counseled them, he sent them out on practice missions. Most basically, he let them live with him and he loved them. He taught them the meaning of love by his love for them; he taught them to take on his mission by his example in carrying it out himself.

The plan of Jesus had such simplicity that we have difficulty understanding it. He focused on preparing a small group of ordinary people who could be the seed, the nucleus of his Church. Jesus brought the message of the Father's love to the disciples; he taught them about love, teaching them above all by his example. All the rest was left in their hands under the power and guidance of the Holy Spirit.

We need to particularly note that Jesus did not write a book. If written words were to be the all-important focus in his Church, we would have expected him to leave us something in writing. Most world leaders put down their vision in writing, but Jesus left no written manifesto behind. Since it would have been easy for him to have done so, we must interpret this as a deliberate choice on his part.

Nor did Jesus choose followers who would make particularly good writers. The scribes, who were the keepers and writers of the word in Judaism, were conspicuously absent from the ranks of the apostles. Fishermen are not generally noted for their literary abilities. Had Jesus placed great emphasis on getting his sermons down accurately in writing, he would have chosen someone to transcribe them, as Jeremiah commissioned Baruch to write down his prophecies. There is no evidence, however, that Jesus did so.

Just as the focus of Jesus was not on political power or cultural enlightenment or large numbers of followers, it was not on the written word. Instead his focus was on the living word: on his word embodied in the lives of a small number of followers, on his word living on in and through them. Under the inspiration of the Holy Spirit, they were to be the nucleus of Christ's Church. They would live the new command of love and be so united among themselves that the world, seeing them, would believe that Jesus Christ was truly the Son of God and through that belief find life. The people of God were to be the word of God.

It is in this context that we can understand the birth of the Church described in the Acts of the Apostles. The Holy Spirit did not create something from nothing: he completed the work that Jesus had begun. Once the apostles had received the outpouring of the Holy Spirit, the Church could come into its full life because of Jesus' years of teaching and preparation.

It is in this context that we can understand how Scripture came to be written for us.

THE HANDING ON

Paul summarized the message he preached as he traveled on his missionary journeys: "Brothers, I want to remind you of the gospel I preached to you, which you received and in which you stand firm.... I handed on to you first of all what I myself received, that Christ died for our sins in accordance with the Scriptures; that he was buried and, in accordance with the Scriptures, rose on the third day; that he was seen by Cephas, then by the Twelve" (1 Cor 15:1, 3-5 NAB).

When Paul spoke of the "Scriptures" here, he was referring to those books that we know as the Old Testament. He was not referring to the written Gospels that we read in the New Testament, for they had not yet been written at the time Paul was writing this first letter to Corinth.

Paul considered his mission to be the "handing on" to others of the message that he himself had received. Other modern translations of Scripture translate Paul's word as "taught" (JB) or "delivered" (RSV). But the Greek word that Paul used is the word which gives us, through its Latin equivalent, the modern word "tradition." Paul told the Corinthians that their faith was based on the message that he himself had received and that he had faithfully handed on to them. And that is the root meaning of "tradition": the handing on of the gospel message.

Jesus Christ brought us the revelation of saving truth from God, and commissioned his apostles to hand it on to others. "Go, therefore, make disciples of all the nations; baptize them in the name of the Father and of the Son and of the Holy Spirit, and teach them to observe all the commands I gave you. And know that I am with you always; yes, to the end of time" (Mt 28:19-20 JB). From the preaching of the apostles, under the power and guidance of the Holy Spirit, the Church began. The apostles were to be those who "handed on" the saving truth of the gospel.

The "handing on" was done exclusively by word-of-mouth preaching for several decades. The first of the books of the New Testament to be written were Paul's letters to Thessalonika, written about twenty years after the resurrection and ascension of Jesus Christ into heaven. None of the Gospels in the form we know them can be dated before about 65 A.D., and the Gospel of John was not written until around the end of the first century. To hear the saving truth about Jesus Christ meant literally to *hear* it. To accept the gospel was to accept the living tradition that was being handed on in the Church.

Thus Paul's letters bristle with references to his verbal handing on of the gospel. "You have done well in remembering me so constantly and in maintaining the traditions just as I passed them on to you" (1 Cor 11:2 JB). "Now we command you, brethren, in the name of our Lord Jesus Christ, that you keep away from any brother who is living in idleness and not in accord with the tradition that you received from us" (2 Thes 3:6 RSV). Paul instructs Timothy to train others to hand on the message: "You have heard everything that I teach in public; hand it on to reliable people so that they in turn will be able to teach others" (2 Tm 2:2 JB).

The books of the New Testament came to be written within the context of the early Christian communities. They were written to meet the needs of the growing Church by setting down the living tradition in writing. As the number of churches that Paul founded grew, he could not meet their needs by his personal presence. Hence he turned to writing them letters, most often to resolve specific problems, offer encouragement in the face of their difficulties, and answer questions which had arisen. Paul considered his letters to carry his authority and to be a part of handing on the gospel tradition: "So then, brethren, stand firm and hold to the traditions which you were taught by us, either by word of mouth or by letter" (2 Thes 2:15 RSV). Paul even intended some of his letters to be passed from one church community to the next (Col 4:16).

The Gospels were committed to writing to preserve this living tradition as its first eyewitnesses, the apostles, began to grow old or suffer martyrdom. Luke the evangelist was not one of the twelve apostles, and had not known Jesus during his life on earth. Luke set out to write down the tradition that was being preached: remembrances of the words of Jesus that were passed on by word of mouth, written fragments containing these sayings, and most likely a copy of Mark's Gospel. Luke began his Gospel by stating this purpose in writing it, addressing himself to a certain "Theophilus":

Seeing that many others have undertaken to draw up accounts of the events that have taken place among us, exactly as these were handed down to us by those who from the outset were eyewitnesses and ministers of the word, I in my turn, after carefully going over the whole story from the beginning, have decided to write an ordered account for you, Theophilus, so that your Excellency may learn how well founded the teaching is that you have received.   Luke 1:1-4 JB

Luke presumed that the gospel was already familiar to those he was writing to and that they were finding life through its words. Written accounts of the gospel were already beginning to appear; Luke wished to do nothing more than to faithfully compile the oral and written tradition into a careful account. He wished to be faithful to what "has been handed down to us."

Under the guidance of the Holy Spirit, the New Testament writers did more than simply try to remember Jesus' every word and deed. From the very outset, the Church had to face new questions and new situations. Even in the years immediately following the resurrection of Jesus, the gospel was not a dead letter, a rigid remembrance of the word that Jesus taught, but a living "handing on," guided by the Holy Spirit, confronting new questions and situations.

The first major crisis affecting the Church was the question of how Gentiles could be admitted to the Church. The ministry of Jesus was largely limited to Jews. On Pentecost day, Jews from many countries came into the Church. But they were still Jews: the whole early Church at that point "went as a body to the Temple every day" (Acts 2:46 JB), that is, to the Jerusalem Temple of the Jews. The earliest Church was a segment of Judaism—a segment that proclaimed Jesus as the Messiah that Israel had awaited. If Gentiles—non-Jews—were to come to faith in Jesus Christ, how should they be received? Should they be required to convert to Judaism first? Should they be bound by the Law of Moses? Should they too worship in the Jewish Temple? Nothing in Christ's explicit teaching seemed to resolve this question.

How this question was settled is one of the dramas underlying the Acts of the Apostles and some of Paul's letters. The solution was found under the guidance of the Holy Spirit—guidance which charted the course that the early Church was to take: "The apostles and elders, your brothers, send greetings to the brothers of pagan birth in Antioch, Syria, and Cilicia.... It has been decided by the Holy Spirit and by ourselves not to saddle you with any burden beyond these essentials" (Acts 15:23, 28 JB).

The needs of the early Church also influenced their remembrance of what Jesus did and taught and what elements were handed on in their teaching. The Gospel of John notes that Jesus worked many signs "not recorded in this book" (Jn 20:30 JB). The Holy Spirit guided the evangelists in selecting material for their renditions of the gospel. The Gospels were not biographies of Jesus written to merely portray his life; they were vehicles of life, shaped in accordance with their purpose. What John wrote was "recorded so that you may believe that Jesus is the Christ, the Son of God, and that believing this you may have life through his name" (Jn 20:31 JB). This life was the life of the Church, the Holy Spirit. The purpose for which the Gospels were written and the context in which they were to be read influenced the shape they took.

Frequently the common prayer life of the early Church, its liturgy, shaped the manner of expressing the gospel. This is seen in the accounts of the Last Supper. Paul wrote to Corinth that "this is what I received from the Lord and in turn passed on to you: that on the same night that he was betrayed, the Lord Jesus took some bread, and thanked God for it and broke it, and he said, 'This is my body, which is for you; do this in memorial of me.' In the same way he took the cup after supper, and said, 'This cup is the new covenant in my blood. Whenever you drink it, do this as a memorial of me'" (1 Cor 11:23-25 JB).

The Lord's Supper was celebrated for several decades before Paul wrote his letters to Corinth, and for even longer before the Gospel accounts of the Last Supper were written. The words of Jesus were remembered in the daily prayer life of the Church, in the "breaking of the bread." Through their constant repetition in the Liturgy, they came to be expressed and remembered in a set way. When Paul wrote to Corinth about the Last Supper, the words he used were the words already in use in the Liturgy of the early Church. When the authors of the Gospels set down the living tradition in writing, these were the words they used, with the slight variations that occurred in the various strands of oral tradition and liturgical custom.

Note what Paul said when he wrote these words to Corinth: "This is what I received from the Lord, and in turn passed on to you." We can understand this as saying, "This is what was handed on to me by the authentic and living tradition of the Church, and this is what I in turn handed on to you and now write to remind you of." Paul's letters were written as reminders of a message that had already been "handed on" by the early Church; they were written "to refresh your memories" (Rom 15:15 JB; consult also 2 Pt 1:12-15).

The needs of the early Church most likely influenced the way the Gospels presented the familiar passage in which the apostles wish to send away the children who were flocking to Jesus. One of the questions faced by the early Church was whether to baptize children or not. The first converts were adults; was baptism to be restricted to adults, or were children also to be baptized? In pondering this question, the Church thought back to the example of Christ. Jesus seemed to set no minimum age for entrance into the kingdom of God. He had welcomed children, despite the apostles' wish to send them away: "Let the little children come to me; do not stop them; for it is to such as these that the kingdom of God belongs" (Mk 10:14 JB).

It seems likely that the example of Jesus in dealing with children was given a particular application to resolve the question of whether children should be admitted to baptism. This incident in the life of Jesus was remembered because it guided the Church in making that decision. As the teaching of Jesus was handed on from person to person, the words already in use in the baptismal liturgy came to be the words used in the retelling of this incident from Jesus' life.

The Greek term used in the Gospel for "do not stop them" is the same Greek term found in the early baptismal liturgy, where it is used to signify that a person should be admitted to baptism. It is also the same Greek phrase that is used in Acts, in the decision to baptize the Ethiopian eunuch (Acts 8:36) and in the decision to baptize Cornelius and the members of his household (Acts 10:47). As in the case of the words of the Eucharist, the liturgical life of the Church influenced the words chosen for use in the Gospels. And the Church's need to resolve the question of baptizing children was an influence for remembering and handing on the incident of Jesus welcoming children to himself.

Sometimes the mere fact of the Church's existence influenced the way the words of Jesus were handed on. "If a brother sins against you, go and tell him his fault.... If he does not listen, take two others along with you.... If he refuses to listen to them, tell it to the *church*" (Mt 18:15, 16, 17 RSV). This teaching of Jesus provided a guide for resolving conflicts between members of the early Church. Its formulation in the Gospel clearly reflects its use within the context of the Church—a Church that did not yet exist during the lifetime of Jesus.

We can hence see that the needs and prayer life of the early Church influenced which incidents and teachings from the life of Jesus were remembered, and influenced the manner in which those incidents were expressed. The incidents and words were handed on by word of mouth long before they were set down in written form. The writing was the final act, but an act which was highly dependent on the verbal handing on of the gospel which had gone before. It was thus highly important that this handing on of the message of salvation was done under the guidance of the Holy Spirit.

THE SPIRIT'S GUIDANCE

We cannot limit the inspiration of Scripture to the final setting down of words in writing; the guidance of the Holy Spirit in shaping the oral tradition was essential. We must not imagine that when the evangelists sat down to write the Gospel accounts they began with nothing, or took faulty remembrances and through the inspiration of the Holy Spirit were able to correct them. The Holy Spirit certainly inspired the writing of the Gospels, but he also inspired the handing on of the gospel message that preceded that writing. His activity in inspiring the one cannot be separated from his activity in inspiring the other.

It is clear that the inspiration of the Holy Spirit is something given to a community of people as well as to individuals. The handing on of the faith was not merely a matter of one inspired person speaking to others, although that was one very important aspect. The reality was much more complex. The Holy Spirit inspired and guided the Church and its leaders in their decisions concerning the admission of Gentiles to baptism, the baptism of children, the development of its forms of worship. The gospel was a living word, incarnated in the life of the Church. Its final writing was as much an expression of the life of the Church as it was a writing down of something which had previously been passed on by word of mouth. From one point of view, it is only a secondary matter that the words of Scripture are inspired. Jesus' promise of the Holy Spirit was much more than a matter of promising that a book would be written which would be free from errors. His promise was that the Spirit would inspire—dwell in and guide—a people, a Church. One aspect of the Spirit's inspiration of the Church was his guiding of the handing on of the message of salvation, and in turn one aspect of that was his guiding of those who set down the oral tradition in writing. Christ did not come to create a holy book but a holy people. The temple of the Holy Spirit is not a book but the body of Christ.

Paul gave us various lists of the ways in which the Holy Spirit is present in the Church, inspiring and guiding his people so that the body of Christ might be built up. "One may have the gift of preaching with wisdom given him by the Spirit; another may have the gift of preaching instruction given him by the same Spirit; and another the gift of faith given by the same Spirit; another again the gift of healing, through this one Spirit; one, the power of miracles; another, prophecy; another the gift of recognizing spirits; another the gift of tongues and another the ability to interpret them" (1 Cor 12:8-10 JB). Another list of Paul's reads differently but has similar meaning: "To some, his gift was that they should be apostles; to some, prophets; to some, evangelists; to some, pastors and teachers; so that the saints together make a unity in the work of service, building up the body of Christ" (Eph 4:11-12 JB).

Paul recognized the Holy Spirit as the one giving the various gifts and roles of service. The presence of the Spirit in the Church was not a vague presence, but a presence concretely manifested through the gifts of service that he gave. These gifts only had meaning in the context of the Christian community; their purpose was the building up of the Church. Paul also insisted that some gifts were more valuable than others, and that the importance of all gifts could be judged by their value for the Church.

The gifts of the Spirit must be seen as an important aspect of the way the Holy Spirit guided the handing on of the gospel message in the early Church. He inspired preachers and teachers before he inspired writers. In fact, Paul does not even mention authors or writers in any of his lists of the ways in which the Spirit operates! We should not take this to mean that the writers of the New Testament were not inspired. They were—including Paul himself when he listed the gifts of the Spirit. The point is that the focus of the Spirit's inspiration was the Church, and that he worked through a variety of gifts to provide for the teaching needs of the Church and the faithful handing on of the message of Jesus.

When we reflect on Jesus' selection and commissioning of the apostles, and on the way the early Church resolved the question of Gentile converts, and on the teaching of Paul in his letters, it is clear that the early Church recognized certain people as authoritative teachers and leaders. A special rank was given to apostles and "elders." It was they who under the guidance of the Holy Spirit ultimately resolved the questions facing the early Church. Apostles and elders were the final touchstone of the authenticity of the handing on of the gospel.

While there was consultation and interaction between the apostles and the early Jerusalem community regarding the need for creating deacons, it was the Twelve who called the community together to deal with the issue, and it was the Twelve who made the decision to ordain deacons (Acts 6:1-6). The Gentile convert question was resolved when "the apostles and elders met to look into the matter" (Acts 15:6 JB); Peter and James played the dominant roles in the meeting. When Paul listed desirable qualities for elders, he said that, along with personal maturity and holiness, an elder "must have a firm grasp of the unchanging message of the tradition, so that he can be counted on for both expounding the sound doctrine and refuting those who argue against it" (Ti 1:9 JB).

Paul's letters also reveal the crosscurrents of thoughts during the years following Christ's ascension into heaven. Not everyone received or understood the gospel in its purity; not everyone handed it on faithfully. Paul was opposed by those who demanded that the entire Mosaic Law be followed by Gentile converts to Christ; he also had to contend with the superstition and pagan practices that new converts carried over into their Christianity. Paul had to warn people not to accept any gospel preached to them that was different from the tradition he had handed on, even if they should hear the new gospel from an angel (Gal 1:8).

A touchstone of authenticity for the true tradition was hence necessary. There could be no appeal to the Bible, for the New Testament had yet to be compiled. Not every prophetic utterance could be accepted without question, for false prophets also claimed to speak by the inspiration of the Spirit (1 Jn 4:1). The touchstone of authenticity was found within the Christian community, in the Church under the guidance of the apostles and elders. It was through them that the Spirit guided the authentic handing on of the gospel of salvation, in whose words alone eternal life was to be found.

The discernment of the Church was above all necessary in sorting out which early writings faithfully captured the living tradition of the Church and which did not. The four Gospels we accept as the inspired Word of God were only four of many writings claiming to be Gospels. Some even claimed to have been written by apostles: the Gospel of Thomas, for example. This work begins by stating, "These are the secret words which the living Jesus spoke and Didymus Judas Thomas wrote." Then follow one hundred fourteen sayings of Jesus, some very similar to the teaching of Jesus found in the four Gospels of the New Testament, but most quite different.

Writings also appeared in the early Church which claimed to be lost letters from Paul or claimed to narrate the acts of the apostles John, Andrew, and Thomas, just as the New Testament book of Acts treats the ministry of Peter and Paul. Even apocalyptic books of revelation appeared, purporting to be revelations given to Peter or Paul or Thomas.

It is easy to see that the early Church faced a problem in sorting out the writings that were an authentic handing on of the gospel message from those that weren't. It was not self-evident which books should be considered sacred Scripture and which should not. The claim that a letter was written by Paul, or that a gospel was written by Thomas, or that a revelation was given to Peter, was not enough to establish that these were indeed apostolic works. And on the other hand, just because a gospel was written by someone other than an apostle did not mean that it was to be rejected; Luke was not one of the twelve apostles.

Far from the New Testament dropping down from heaven to be the constitution and bylaws of the early Church, it was the early Church who constituted the New Testament. The individual books of the New Testament were written to set down in words the authentic faith that the early Church was already living, the faith that had been handed on under the guidance of the Holy Spirit. And it was the Church that decided which of the many books in circulation claiming to be apostolic writings were really such. It was the Church that decided which books could be used as a standard to judge the authenticity of preaching. Our word "canon" comes from a Semitic word which meant a reed used for measuring. A "canonical" book is one that can be accepted as a measure, a guide, a rule.

We have no evidence that there was ever a special revelation from God directly establishing the books to be accepted as canonical—as inspired writings that could serve as the guide for the faith of the Church. Rather, it was the bishops of the Church who decided which books were to be considered a part of the Bible. The leaders of the Church made this decision after much debate, and they made it with the guidance of the Holy Spirit. But it was the teaching authority of the Church which settled the issue and selected twenty-seven books as an authentic expression of the faith of the Church, rejecting as apocryphal well over one hundred others.

The debate over which books were to be accepted as canonical and read as the word of God lasted several hundred years. During this time, different lists of inspired books were accepted in different parts of the Church. While there was general agreement about most of the books we read as part of the New Testament, there were a number of books that caused considerable discussion—for instance, the letter to the Hebrews. It was not until around the year 400 that complete agreement prevailed throughout the Church that the twenty-seven books we read as the New Testament were indeed the inspired word of God, and no others.

IT IS THE CHURCH WHO LISTENS

John states in his first letter that the reason he is writing is so "that which we have seen and heard we proclaim also to you, so that you may have fellowship with us; and our fellowship is with the Father and with his Son Jesus Christ" (1 Jn 1:3 RSV). Fellowship with the Father through Jesus Christ is inextricably linked with fellowship with other Christians, with being a part of the body of Christ.

God chose to speak to us not as a voice out of the clouds, but through human words: words formed by human lips, words set down in writing by human hands. God chose to save us not as individuals, but as a part of the body of Christ. The work of the Holy Spirit within us enables us to address God as Father and to graft us onto the body of Christ. To be made a son or daughter of God is to join the family of God.

Revelation began with the dialogue between God and his people in Old Testament times; revelation reached its fulfillment in Jesus Christ, the Word made flesh. The word of God was nurtured and handed on in the people of God. The word of God today still finds its home in the people of God. Scripture is part of the continuing dialogue between God and his people, the Church.

Scripture must be read as it was written: as an expression of faith within the Church. Our faith and our membership in the body of Christ are the basis for reading Scripture. The words of Scripture have full meaning only for someone joined to Christ through his body. We do not merely read Scripture as individuals; we also participate in the Church's reading of Scripture, as one aspect of its life. This can be seen most clearly in the proclamation of Scripture during the Liturgy—a proclamation that is an event within the Church, an event which nourishes its life.

That the Church is the place where we listen to the word of God is not universally understood or accepted. Some hold that the Bible is the primary way that God speaks to us, placing it apart from the Church and above the Church. Others go even further, saying that the Bible is all that is needed, that all that is important is our relationship with Jesus Christ, and that the Church itself is unnecessary.

Such views are unsupported by the Bible itself. The thrust of the Gospels is that Jesus worked to leave behind a group that would be his body. His focus was not on writing a book or even on selecting those who would primarily be authors. The Acts of the Apostles focuses on the spread of the Church, not on the development of the Bible. The way to salvation was found through becoming part of the apostolic Church.

The Bible does not teach that "all you need is the Bible," even though a passage is sometimes quoted to support this view:

> You must keep to what you have been taught and know to be true; remember who your teachers were, and how, ever since you were a child, you have known the holy Scriptures—from these you can learn the wisdom that leads to salvation through faith in Christ Jesus. All Scripture is inspired by God and can profitably be used for teaching, for refuting error, for guiding people's lives and teaching them to be holy. This is how the man who is dedicated to God becomes fully equipped and ready for any good work.   2 Timothy 3:14-17 JB

Timothy is advised that it is highly profitable to read Scripture. But he is clearly not told "Scripture is all you need." The Scriptures referred to here are the books that we read as the Old Testament. It would be unthinkable for Paul to claim that the Old Testament provides all we need to know about God and should be considered to be the law of our lives. And it is clear that only the Old Testament is discussed here, for reference is made to Timothy's having read Scripture ever since childhood.

Since Timothy was old enough to be a companion of Paul at the time Paul wrote his first epistle (1 Thessalonians, around 51 A.D.: cf. 1 Thes 1:1), Timothy must have been born at the latest around 30 A.D. The Scriptures that Timothy knew from childhood could hardly have been the writings of the New Testament since he was already an adult when they were written.

We need the guidance of the Church in order to properly read and understand Scripture. We need to be in contact with the understanding of the message of salvation that reaches back to the time of the apostles, and which was expressed in the written words of the Bible. We need the guidance of the Church and the Holy Spirit in bringing the message of Scripture to bear on new situations and new questions.

Interpretation of Scripture must take place with the guidance of the Holy Spirit in the Church. "No one can interpret any prophecy of Scripture by himself. For it was not through any human whim that men prophesied of old; men they were, but, impelled by the Holy Spirit, they spoke the words of God" (2 Pt 1:19-20 NEB). The argument seems to be that just as the prophecy contained in Scripture does not originate with human beings but with the Holy Spirit, so its interpretation is not left up to the individual. The way in which the word of God was uttered to the human race provides the context for our understanding it. God spoke through his people in both Old and New Testament times; our listening and understanding must take place within the context of his people today.

The Holy Spirit is as much in the Church today as he was in the early Church. He did not guide the Council of Jerusalem in deciding the Gentile convert question and then abandon the Church, no longer guiding it through its councils today. Nor does he, now that the Bible has been written, restrict his guidance to the written words of Scripture. He continues to be present in the Church, inspiring the handing on of the message of salvation.

Acceptance of Scripture as the word of God implies acceptance of the way in which it came to be uttered in human language. Acceptance of Scripture implies acceptance of the tradition which formed Scripture and judged it to be inspired. Acceptance of Scripture implies acceptance of the teaching authority of the Church, since it is through that teaching authority that the words of Scripture were judged to be the authentic measure of our faith. We cannot accept an authoritative teaching role for the Church in the first century but deny it that same role today. To do so would be to claim that the Holy Spirit who guided the early Church no longer guides the Church in our time.

The role of the Church is not to pass judgment on the truth or falsity of what is contained in Scripture, but to be nourished by Scripture, to proclaim the message contained in Scripture, and to embody the realities set down there. The role of the Church is to continue the handing on of the message of salvation begun in the time of the apostles. Scripture is a norm for the Church in doing this, as well as a tool. Like Paul, the Church does not merely hand on a message; it hands on life by reconciling us to God through Christ: "It is all God's work. It was God who reconciled us to himself through Christ and gave us the work of handing on this reconciliation" (2 Cor 5:18 JB).

The Church is not like a supreme court, offering definitive interpretations of laws given by a heavenly lawmaker. The Church is an ordered community. Its focus must be on its life and on spreading that life. Sometimes, an authoritative interpretation of the words of Scripture must be made, but in actual practice, that is only one small part of the Church's use of Scripture. We learn much more about Scripture from the way the Church uses it in prayer, for example, than we do from official pronouncements issued with great solemnity. We learn about the meaning of Scripture for our lives by being a full part of the life of the Church.

While the authoritative role of the Church's teaching ministry is essential and provides a necessary base, it is rather in the full life of the Church that our reading of Scripture finds its context and meaning. To reduce the Church to being merely a teacher, however infallible, is to focus on only one dimension of a much larger reality. It is not only what the Church teaches but how the

Church lives that provides the norm for our understanding of Scripture. Our understanding of Scripture is formed in a thousand imperceptible ways: by the preaching we hear, by our common life of worship, by our "fellowship of the Holy Spirit" (2 Cor 13:13) with other Christians.

To take a trivial example: there has never been a formal decree that Paul's words, "In every place, then, I want the men to lift their hands reverently in prayer" (1 Tm 2:8 JB), are not to be taken literally, as a guide for proper prayer. But praying with uplifted arms is not a normal experience for most congregations today. Our style of prayer is more often formed by experience than through explicit teaching or interpretation of Scripture verses.

Admittedly, popular teachings sometimes form us in a less than fully accurate understanding of Scripture. The warning of Jesus in the Gospels that "it is easier for a camel to pass through the eye of a needle than for a rich man to enter the Kingdom of God" (Lk 18:25 JB) has often been explained by asserting that there was a small gate in the city walls of Jerusalem that was called the "Needle's Eye," and that camels could only squeeze through it with difficulty. This interpretation, however, was invented sometime in the Middle Ages; no evidence has ever been found that such a gate existed or that Jesus was referring to such a gate. We must confront the full force of Jesus' warning about wealth, relying upon his promise that "things that are impossible for men are possible for God" (Lk 18:27 JB) rather than upon a popular interpretation which waters down the message of the gospel.

It may be easier to ascribe an otherworldly perfection to the Bible and place all our credence in it, rather than trust in a Church whose human imperfections and sinfulness can be so apparent. But God's plan was not to guide us by writing a perfect book; his plan was to incorporate us into a people on the road to full salvation. Our scandal that the Church is not more perfect was probably felt in the first century; Peter probably never appeared to be flawless. It may be easier to put our faith in Scripture rather than in the Church, but such faith, if it chooses

Scripture over against the Church, is misplaced: it makes Scripture out to be more and the Church to be less than they are in the plan of God.

While the Church is not above the authority of Scripture, the Church does have the authority to proclaim and interpret Scripture. The handing on of the faith is the work of the Church. The Bible is the book of the Church. The handing on of faith cannot be separated from the Church, nor can the Bible be divorced from the Church. The Church must consider the Bible to be "canonical": the rule, the measure, the norm of faith. The preaching and teaching of the Church must be nourished by the Scripture.

It is the Church who listens to the word of God spoken through the Scriptures. God speaks his word to the Church so that the Church itself might be the messenger of God to the world, and the message of God to the world. The word that God spoke in Jesus Christ continues to resound through the world through the lives of those who have found life in his name. The Word of God is now made present in the people of God, the Church.

Part III

Abiding in the Word

EIGHT

As You Continue Reading

THE VARIETY OF SCRIPTURE

S INCE THE WORD OF GOD is given to us as spiritual food, we
should not be surprised to find that it comes in as many vari-
eties as natural food. Life would be dull indeed if all we ate was
oatmeal three times a day, day after day, even if it were specially
enriched oatmeal that provided a nutritionally sound diet.
Instead, we are glad to have the great variety of foods that God
has given us to eat and the great variety of ways in which they
can be prepared.

Scripture comes in a similar variety. The Psalms are quite different from the historical books of the Old Testament, and they
in turn from the oracles of the prophets. Paul's letters are quite
different from the Gospels, and they in turn from the Book of
Revelation. They are all God's word to us, yet a word spoken in
a great variety of ways. Our spiritual life would be much poorer
if every book of the Bible were exactly like every other.

It is tempting to believe that if the Bible is the word of God,
then every word of it must be equally holy and worthy of our
attention. However, once we have made some progress in reading the Bible we discover that some portions of it seem to have
much less to say to us than other portions. Some passages of
Scripture do not seem to have any relevance to us, and we may
even find ourselves bored as we read them. We might not admit
to ourselves that we are bored, however; it would seem disre-

spectful to be bored by a word that God thought worth speaking to us.

There is no use, however, pretending that we find every page of Scripture vitally interesting if we do not. Even if we can fool ourselves, we can't fool God. What is more, he might not expect us to find every verse equally important. He might be quite understanding if we admit that some passages do not hold our interest very long and seem to lack application in our lives.

I believe that our reading of Scripture should be selective, and that we should pay more attention to those passages which do have a clear message for us than to passages which seemingly lack such a message. Rather than strain to extract a message from, for example, the second set of sanctuary and ritual instructions in Exodus 35-40 or the lengthy "Oracles against the Nations" in Jeremiah 46-51, such sections should be read quickly and greater attention paid to the remaining chapters of these books or to the Gospels and letters of the New Testament.

I believe that all of Scripture is worth reading—but some parts are more worth reading than others and should have a greater claim on our time. I also believe that we should be slow to dismiss any section of Scripture as pointless. But that is not to say that its point will necessarily be clear to me now. And rather than get bogged down reading chapters which seem to lack meaning for us at the time, I think it is preferable to devote more attention to those chapters which more clearly speak God's word to us.

On the other hand, just as we eat various foods in order to have a balanced diet, so we need to read all the various kinds of Scripture for a balanced spiritual life. To focus exclusively on one section of the Bible is to miss out on much that Scripture can teach us. But just as we cook or prepare different kinds of foods in different ways in order to best enhance their nutritional value and taste, so we can read different books of the Bible in different ways, in order to best draw out their meaning for us.

Some books we may have to study, particularly the first time we read them. We may have to make use of a commentary, and we might well find our reading a spiritually dry experience. By contrast, our reading of more familiar books of the Bible, particularly the Gospels, can be done more simply, and we will usually have a more immediate sense of God speaking to us in a personal way. Some books of the Bible we can read more rapidly, in big chunks; other books require slow reading, with pauses for meditation. After finishing reading some books, we will find that we have learned a lot; after reading other books, we will find that we have prayed a lot.

We might even want to experiment with reading Scripture aloud. When we learned to read in school, we were taught to read without moving our lips so that we might read faster. That is probably how we read the Bible today: silently, to ourselves. In the ancient world, however, Scripture was normally read out loud, even if a person was reading only for himself or herself.

For example, the Book of Acts tells of the deacon Philip going out on the road from Jerusalem to Gaza, where he sees an Ethiopian riding in a chariot and reading Scripture. "So Philip ran to him, and *heard* him reading Isaiah the prophet" (Acts 8:30). Philip heard him reading Isaiah because the Ethiopian was reading out loud.

The custom of reading Scripture aloud persisted for many centuries. In his *Confessions*, written around 400 A.D., St. Augustine speaks of visiting St. Ambrose and finding him reading the Bible silently. This strikes Augustine as being enough out of the ordinary that he hazards some guesses why Ambrose might be doing such a thing—an indication that Scripture was still normally read out loud (*The Confessions*, Book 6, chapter 3).

Reading Scripture aloud has benefits for us today. It can help us notice things that we might miss if we read the same passage silently. Reading aloud can help a passage come alive for us by more thoroughly involving us in it. Reading out loud also forces us to read more slowly, which in turn helps us grasp its meaning.

We should not be ashamed of stumbling and mispronouncing words when we read aloud; we are not trying to win an award for dramatic reading. Our attention should be on the text rather than on how we sound. We might be self-conscious the first few times we try it, but it will probably become easier for us the more we do it. (If it doesn't, then stop doing it; reading aloud should help us, not be a new burden.)

Some books of the Bible are more suited for reading aloud than others: the poetic passages of the prophets more than the historical books of the Old Testament, for example. The Psalms are the best suited of all Scripture for reading aloud since they were composed to be sung or recited.

DIFFICULTIES IN READING SCRIPTURE

I sometimes find that when I finish reading a passage of Scripture I have no idea what it meant and no very vivid memory of what I read. This sometimes happens when I am reading a difficult portion of the Bible and it also sometimes happens when I am reading a very familiar passage. In the first case, because the passage is difficult, my eyes can skim over the words without any meaning entering into my brain; in the second case, because the words are so familiar, my mind skips ahead of my eyes and reaches the end of the passage first. In both cases, I find myself reading without the words of Scripture making any impression on me or speaking to me as God's word.

I've found three ways of coping with this problem.

First of all, I remind myself that there is no merit in reading words that I do not understand. If I breeze through a chapter without paying much attention to what it says, I might as well not have read it. Therefore if I find myself reading words mechanically I stop, go back to the beginning, and reread them slowly, trying to be more attentive to their meaning. Much of my Scripture reading is therefore rereading, because I missed the point the first time through. Sometimes I have to reread a second or third time.

Second, the most common reason for my reading without understanding is that I am distracted and really trying to do two things at once: read the Bible and think about something else. The cure for this is to put distractions and preoccupations out of my mind as much as possible and resolve not to be doing anything but reading Scripture during my Scripture reading.

Third, sometimes a difficult passage will make more sense in a different translation. I sometimes reread a passage in a second or third translation if I am baffled by what it means. This doesn't always help (sometimes the passage is obscure in every translation), but it quite often throws a fresh light on a perplexing passage.

If angels read Scripture, they probably read it with rapt attention every day, instantly understanding its meaning and lifting their whole beings to God in prayer. But since they already see God face-to-face, they probably do not need to make use of the intermediary of his word in the Bible.

Those of us who are not angels, however, will probably not read the Bible with an equal sense of fulfillment every day. There are days when God seems to speak directly to us through the words of Scripture, when our minds are filled with insight and awe, when our hearts are deeply touched by God's presence. And there are days when none of these things seem to happen, and we think we might as well have been reading the classified ad section of the newspaper for all the good our reading apparently did us. These days probably come more often when we are reading some of the more difficult books of the Old Testament than when we are reading the Gospels or our other favorite books of the New Testament.

Even on difficult days, we should read anyway. Just because one day's reading does not seem to have the same immediate effect on us as another day's does not mean that our reading has been in vain. Even the least rewarding books of the Bible convey something of God's revelation to us and prepare us to better understand the rest of Scripture.

Scripture reading is like marriage: there are days when the duties of marriage and family life outweigh the thrill, but they are a part of marriage and form the background for those times when husband and wife do experience the deep blessings of having been given to each other. The blessings of marriage are based on the faithfulness, come what may, of husband and wife to each other.

So too our Scripture reading: the blessings we receive depend on our faithfulness.

We are sure to find obscure passages when we read the Bible, particularly when we read a book like Genesis. Sometimes we will not be able to make much sense out of what we read, at least not without some kind of help. The ceremony described in Genesis 15 whereby God sealed a covenant with Abraham must strike us as odd, until we discover that this was the way contracts were solemnized in the days before notary publics. On the other hand, the first four verses of chapter six of Genesis may continue to be obscure for us even after we have studied them, and to seemingly lack any implications for our lives today.

When we encounter such perplexities, we should keep in mind that we read the Bible for what we can understand of it, not for what we cannot understand. We read it as God's word to us, a word that is for the most part quite clear and understandable. We should not let puzzling over difficulties occupy most of our time or attention. When we read Scripture we should focus on what we do understand and peacefully consign what we do not understand to a secondary place. We should not let obscurities and puzzles distract us from what we should be paying the most attention to: the word of God speaking to us through what we do understand.

SPECIAL VERSES

Even those chapters of Scripture that seem most obscure or pointless to us after all our efforts will most often contain a verse or group of verses that do have special meaning for us. We may be reading along, doing our best to understand what we read, when a verse will leap out at us, or at least strike us as significant. We may have the sense that this particular verse was written with us in mind; we may have the sense that this verse particularly addresses something in our lives today.

We should be grateful for such special verses and pay particular attention to them. I usually mark them in the margin with pencil as I am doing my daily reading, and then return to these verses when I am done reading, to reflect on them and make them a part of my prayer that day. In my experience, almost every chapter of the Bible contains something that speaks God's particular word to me today, if I am but attentive to it.

Reading the Bible for its overall meaning is important, but so is reading it for its particular meaning for us today. Those verses that strike us in a special way each day can convey God's word to us, as the message we need to hear and treasure that day. Pay attention to them!

There is even an advantage to memorizing these special verses as we find them. Many Christians have committed entire blocks of the Bible to memory—a feat that is beyond me. But I believe it is worthwhile to selectively memorize some verses from Scripture. The most important verses of Scripture for us to memorize will be those that have special meaning for us, either because they contain a very important truth or revelation or because they seem to have particular application to our lives or, hopefully, both. And the easiest verses to memorize will be those that seem to speak to us directly, that seem to convey God's word addressed specifically to us.

I have always had a hard time memorizing anything, but find that there are certain Scripture verses that stick in my memory. They are lodged there because they have special meaning for me and have served as guideposts in my life. I did not make a special effort to memorize them, but I read and pondered on their meaning often enough that their words are a part of me. They now come to mind as I am praying or thinking or sometimes simply as I am letting my mind wander. They remind me of the truths on which I have tried to base my life.

Whatever systems of formal or informal memorization we use, the goal should be the same: to have available in our minds those verses of Scripture that are the truths we live by, so that they can spontaneously be a part of our thoughts and prayers.

One advantage of memorizing certain verses from the Bible is that we can use these verses to counter temptation. There is a certain sameness to our temptations. We usually battle the same old sins and weaknesses year after year, making progress on some fronts while barely holding our own on others. We may be prone to fears and anxiety, and consequently find it difficult to really trust in God's care for us. We may be moody and irritable, and make life unpleasant for those who live with us. We may have a stubborn streak of selfishness in us that taints our attitudes and actions.

We need to employ all the weapons we can in our battle against our ingrained failings: prayer, unceasing effort, prayer for healing, penance. One weapon that we can add to our arsenal is Scripture—verses from the Bible that address our specific sins and strengthen us against our chronic temptations. There are often Scripture verses that match up with our specific situation and speak the precise word of God we need to hear.

For example, if our temptation is to sacrifice everything on the altar of our jobs, Jesus' words, "What profit would there be for one to gain the whole world and forfeit his (or her) life?" (Mt 16:26), may be the message we need to reflect on. If we are anxious, perhaps a verse from Romans 8 might be the encouraging word for us. If we are proud about our accomplishments as a Christian, Jesus' words, "You did not choose me, no I chose you" (Jn 15:16), might help us gain perspective. At one point in my life, when a particular Christian service threatened to be more of a burden than I could bear, I used a verse from 1 Peter as a weapon against despair: "For to this you have been called, just as Christ suffered for you, leaving you an example that you should follow in his steps" (1 Pt 2:21).

Sometimes verses that have special meaning for us will jump out at us as we go about our Bible reading. Sometimes we can find them by searching for them. However we discover them, we need to remember them so that we can call them to mind when we are in the midst of battle.

SMALL GROUP SHARING

Jesus addresses us as individuals when we read his word in Scripture. His word is a personal word to us, a message which is no less personal for also being a message to others. But Jesus also wants to address his word to us as his followers gathered together in his name. He wants to speak his word to us not only through the words of the Bible as we read them but through one another's words as we share what Scripture means to us.

Jesus promised, "Where two or three meet in my name, I shall be there with them" (Mt 18:20 JB). Jesus is made present in a very definite way when we share our lives as Christians with each other. When we tell others how we have heard the word of God addressed to us we help them hear the word that is spoken to them.

A Bible sharing group can be set up quite simply. As few as four people who meet regularly can make up a successful Scripture sharing group, although six to eight is a better number. The faithfulness of people's attendance and the openness with which they share are more important than striving for any particular number. Most groups find that weekly meetings work best, although some groups set their meetings for every two weeks.

Different meeting formats can be used to provide a framework for sharing. It is usually best to have one person designated as the leader of the meeting. This might be a different person each week, or one person might be the leader for an extended period of time. The meeting should begin and end with prayer. Many groups make these times opportunities for informal shared prayer, with each person feeling free to pray aloud in their own words. If a group is not comfortable with this style of prayer, the leader should lead the group in a form of prayer that they can enter into wholeheartedly.

In a Scripture sharing group, the leader does not have to function as an expert, able to answer everyone's questions about the Bible. Rather, the role of the leader is to help the members of the group share with each other, keeping the discussion focused on the Bible. This might mean encouraging the quieter members to share more and the more vocal members to listen more (to be done tactfully!). Or it might mean bringing the group back to the words of Scripture if the discussion goes too far afield. Once in a while the leader might have to end a line of discussion and begin a new one, if the group has come up against a point of interpretation they cannot agree upon.

The main attention of a Scripture sharing group should be on the words of Scripture as they speak to the lives of the participants of the group. The meeting should not be a discussion about Scripture in the abstract; it should be a sharing of what Scripture means in the life of each member of the group. Sometimes it is helpful for a member of the group to say something about the historical background of a Scripture passage in order that everyone might understand it better, or to share something he or she read about a passage that helped them understand its meaning. But the focus of the group should be on personal discussion of their Christian lives as addressed by the word of God.

Some groups share about a common passage that they have all read; other groups base their sharing on whatever Scripture each member has read in the past week. If the discussion is to be about one passage, it is best to have that passage read aloud by one member of the group and then pause for a time of silent reflection and listening. Sometimes reading the passage aloud a second or third time later in the meeting will provide an opportunity for hearing God speak more strongly through it and will spark a new depth of discussion.

After the passage has been read and there have been a few moments of silent reflection, the leader can initiate the sharing by asking such questions as, "What was the author of this passage of Scripture trying to convey to the reader at that time?" "How do you understand these words to apply to your life?" "Does anyone think that God is addressing these words to them in a particular way?"

It should be expected that a group will grow in its ability to share as its members grow to know and love each other. A group that might start with rather restrained sharing and occasional awkward silences may soon find that discussion flows freely and the meeting time passes quickly.

Meetings should initially be scheduled to last about an hour and a half, and then later tailored to the group's needs and interests. It is often desirable to have light refreshments at the end, so that purely social sharing can be held off until that time. It is better to have a shorter set time for Scripture sharing that is adhered to than a long or indefinite meeting time that allows wandering off onto other topics.

There is also a second type of small group Scripture meeting, a type that could be called a Bible study group. In a study group the aim is to learn more about the Bible itself, in contrast to a sharing group where the aim is to share what the Bible means for our lives. A study group needs more resources to be successful.

The ideal for a study group is to have as a leader someone who can teach the group and answer questions. If such a person is not available, then the group could listen to a series of audio- or videotapes and discuss them. Or the group could make use of one of the packaged programs of Scripture study which are available today, such as the Little Rock program. Or the group could read and discuss some book about the Bible, treating it as a textbook. While study groups do require more resources and work than sharing groups, they also give their members a greater depth of understanding of Scripture, and lay the groundwork for better sharing of Scripture.

NINE

Some Problems
of Interpretation

T HE BIBLE IS BOTH A BOOK OF LIFE for us, and a book of a lifetime. There will be no end to the additional meaning and insight we get from it as we read; there will be no end to our listening to the Lord speak to us through its words, short of our listening to him directly when we see him face-to-face.

It should not bewilder or discourage us, then, if there are portions of the Bible that we do not understand or if there are questions we do not know how to answer. Our continued reading and study will bring us greater insight, and the problem areas should gradually diminish. The Bible explains itself: our increased familiarity with Scripture will provide the context for understanding the more difficult or obscure books of Scripture. Reading books about the Bible is also an indispensable help, if we are to journey from twentieth-century Western patterns of thought back several thousand years to Hebrew patterns of thought and manners of expression.

Yet we should not be surprised if difficulties still remain, if some passages still perplex us. The second letter of Peter makes reference to the difficulty of understanding Paul's writings (2 Pt 3:16)—and if an inspired writer had difficulty understanding Paul, our own struggles should not be unexpected.

Problems of interpretation and application can arise for every book of the Bible. It is obviously beyond the scope of this book to address them all, much less resolve them. However, three problem areas can be discussed—three areas that often cause difficulty.

One particular question seems to most often bother the modern reader of Scripture: the historicity of the Bible. This question can take many forms: "Did Adam and Eve really live?" "Did all the miracles mentioned in the New Testament really happen?" It also confronts the reader in a more subtle way, with the questions, "Was Jesus really as the Gospels portray him? Are his actual words recorded in the New Testament?"

One approach to Scripture would attempt to settle these questions with dispatch: "The Bible is the inspired word of God; therefore everything it states must be true. If it says that it rained for forty days and forty nights, then it *did* rain for forty days and forty nights."

Such an uncomplicated and literal belief in the words of the Bible is unfortunately difficult to maintain. The history of simple, literal interpretation of the Bible is a history of steady erosion. None of us today would side with Galileo's accusers, who condemned him for maintaining that the earth revolved around the sun in apparent contradiction to the statement of the Book of Joshua that "the sun stood still" in its revolution around the earth (Jos 10:12-14).

If our interpretation of the Bible is subject to steady erosion, we may worry that our faith is eroding away too. It can be very unsettling to believe something as "an article of faith" one year and find it questioned or denied by theologians the next year. When absolute certainty is lacking, what is one to believe? In particular, "if we can't believe the Bible, what can we believe?"

This problem becomes most acute when it seems to affect the central truths of our faith, when it seems to affect our understanding of Jesus Christ. We may be able to revise our thinking of some Old Testament incidents without grave difficulties, but any revision in our understanding of Jesus and his message to us is another matter. We need to believe that the Gospels contain the gospel truth.

Let us examine three different parts of the Bible, and explore the type of truth that they contain. Should the opening pages of Genesis be considered a historical account of the creation of the world? How faithfully do the Gospels present Jesus Christ to us? How literally should we interpret the Book of Revelation?

GENESIS 1-11

The first eleven chapters of the Book of Genesis tell of the creation of the world and the lives of people before the time of Abraham. These chapters have caused considerable debate in the past: debate over the origin of "original sin," debate over the theory of evolution, debate over the creation and age of the universe. There has been debate over the kind of fruit Eve handed Adam, and people have gone on expeditions looking for the ark in which Noah survived the flood.

One interpretation of the first chapters of Genesis would insist that since they are the inspired word of God, they are to be read as a literal and true account of the creation of the world and the lives of the first human beings. Some have dated the creation of the world at 4004 B.C. by adding up the ages of the people and generations that came between Adam and Christ.

An opposite reaction is to label the whole creation account nonsense, pointing out that scientists date the age of the universe in billions of years and date the origins of the human race in hundreds of thousands of years. A potential conflict between science and revelation emerges. Some Christians still consider the theory of evolution to be directly contradicted by the Bible and protest when it is taught to their children in public schools.

To understand the first eleven chapters of Genesis (as in understanding the whole Bible), it is necessary to determine what the inspired author wanted to teach. In order to determine this, we must have some insight into the literary form that the author used. Just as we must understand the parables of Jesus as parables (and not demand that an actual robbery occurred on the Jericho road, to use our previous example), so we must read Genesis 1-11 for the particular kind of writing that it is. Knowing the purpose for which these chapters were written and the context in which they were written will help us understand what they are meant to teach us today.

The Old Testament was the collected books of the chosen people. It was an expression of their heritage, of their life as a people chosen and guided by God. It was a collection of books that they began to write and assemble only after God made his covenant with them on Mount Sinai.

The history of the chosen people begins, properly speaking, with the second book of the Bible, the Book of Exodus. Exodus begins with the descendants of Abraham living in Egypt as a slave class and describes how Moses was selected by God to lead them to freedom. These events marked the beginning of their life as God's chosen people.

Events that happened before the time of Moses were preserved as family memories: memories of Abraham leaving his native country and journeying to Canaan some six hundred years before the Exodus; memories of Isaac and Jacob; memories of the twelve sons of Jacob and their migration with their families to Egypt. A promise had been made to Abraham by God, a promise sealed with a solemn covenant. But this early covenant only found its full expression and meaning with the covenant made on Mount Sinai.

But what of events that occurred before the time of Abraham? The Israelites preserved no memories, strictly speaking, of these events. Their family heritage began with their father Abraham. Still, it was desirable to preface the retelling of the Exodus with an introduction, an account of the beginnings of humankind up to the time of the Exodus. This prefatory introduction is the Book of Genesis—a book about the beginnings as its name would suggest.

The Book of Genesis falls into two parts. The first eleven chapters tell of the earliest beginnings; the remaining chapters retell the family histories of Abraham, Isaac, Jacob, Joseph, and the migration to Egypt. Both parts set the scene for the Book of Exodus: the first eleven chapters by telling of the origins of the human race; the remainder of the book by preserving the Israelites' memories of their distant forefather Abraham and of how they came to live in Egypt.

Although the Book of Genesis comes first in the Bible, it was not necessarily the first book to be written. Nor was it written a chapter at a time, as the events it describes occurred. The incidents contained in Genesis were first told by word of mouth, and only later set down in writing. Nor were all the oral traditions set down in writing at once: the Book of Genesis was written and edited by stages.

Some parts of Genesis were apparently written and compiled in Judah around the time of David or Solomon, about the tenth or ninth centuries B.C. A slightly different set of oral traditions appear to have been compiled in writing a little bit later in Israel, the Northern Kingdom. Sometime after the fall of the Northern Kingdom in 721 B.C., these two documents were edited together. Still later, after the return from exile in the sixth century B.C., another strand of the written tradition was added, and the Book of Genesis as we know it received its final editing. Although the traditions it preserves go back to the time of Abraham, and although some written fragments might date back to the time of Moses, the actual writing and compilation of Genesis occurred in stages between the tenth and fifth centuries before Christ.

This explains why many of the incidents in Genesis are told more than once and in slightly different ways. There are two accounts of the creation of the world. The first account, which extends up to chapter two, verse 4, is from the tradition that found its way into writing after the time of the exile. The second account, from 2:4 to 3:24, was compiled in writing at the time of David or Solomon some four hundred years earlier. Similarly, there are two interwoven accounts of the flood in chapters six to eight, one describing a flood of forty days, the other a flood of one hundred fifty days (Gn 7:17, 24).

The authors of Genesis drew on family memories passed down from generation to generation for their accounts of Abraham, Isaac, Jacob, and his sons. For the accounts of the creation of the world and the beginnings of man and woman, they could not draw on such memories. No human beings had been present at the creation of the universe; even the stories of the first humans would not have been handed down through the long centuries that people lived before Abraham. Abraham's ancestors had not worshipped Yahweh, but had served other gods (Jos 24:2). They would not have transmitted any memories of the one true God's previous interventions with humankind, even had such memories otherwise survived the centuries. Nor is there any evidence that God made a special revelation to the writers of Genesis to instruct them in these events that they would otherwise have had no knowledge of.

Rather, the origin of the first eleven chapters of Genesis must be found in the stories of creation that were common in the Near East at the time that the content of Genesis was evolving. Archaeologists have discovered several Mesopotamian accounts of the creation of the world, of the origins of the human race, of a great flood. What we read in the first eleven chapters of Genesis displays many similarities with these legends or myths—and several key differences. The chosen people did not simply adopt the popular accounts of creation that were in circulation in their part of the world; they changed and adapted those accounts to make them vehicles of God's revelation.

Rather than showing our world generated by a number of different gods, as the myths usually did, Genesis presents the one true God as the source of all that is. Instead of depicting a great flood sent because of the irrational anger of the gods (as in Mesopotamian myths), Genesis shows a flood sent by God because of humanity's sin and corruption. Only in the Bible is the creation of the human race described as God breathing his own divine breath into them. While there are similarities between the accounts in Genesis and ancient myths, there are also unmistakable differences. It is in these differences that God's revelation is chiefly to be found.

An old saying has it that the Bible teaches "not how the heavens go, but how to go to heaven." The first part of Genesis does not contain a revelation from God about the age of the universe, about the relationship of the earth to the sun and other celestial bodies, or about the life expectancy of early humans. It does teach that the material world comes from the hand of God, that God specially intervened to create the human race, that humanity was meant for friendship with God, that the human race rejected God, that their rejection of God is the cause of suffering, that God still holds out hope of reconciliation for the human race and has not abandoned them. The vehicle Genesis uses to teach these truths are stories adapted from the popular culture of the time. But the revelation contained in them is something not found in the popular stories; it is rather a revelation the chosen people had learned from their covenant relationship with God. We must remember that Genesis was written well after God revealed himself to Israel through Moses and that its understanding of God reflects this.

The inevitable question must be faced: can we read the first eleven chapters of Genesis as being scientific and historical truth or not? If we mean by this, can we read Genesis as we would a modern science or history book, the answer is clearly no. God was not trying to reveal scientific truths. Genesis neither proves nor disproves any theory of evolution. The theory of evolution might be right or wrong, but the issue is a scientific one, not a scriptural one.

But if we ask, can we read the first part of Genesis as God's revelation to us, the answer is yes. God does reveal something of himself, something of the origins of the world and of the human race, something of humanity's sinfulness, something of the root causes of suffering in these chapters. His revelation of these matters is not complete in Genesis, and we must interpret it in the light of the teaching of the whole Bible. But it does contain God's revelation to us. It contains it in a literary form that we might be uncomfortable with; we might wish that God had somehow worked things out to provide us with a scientific and historical account. But this is not the form of revelation we have been given. We can neither dismiss the first eleven chapters of Genesis as childish fairy tales, nor read them as scientific historical documents. We can read them as containing God's revelation to us, presented in an imaginative way but containing truths nonetheless.

Our reading of Genesis should be done with an edition of the Bible that contains good explanatory notes, perhaps which point out where different strands of written and oral traditions have been woven together. For those interested in a scholarly study of Genesis, Bruce Vawter's *On Genesis* can be recommended. Once we have a basic understanding of how God's revelation is given to us through the Book of Genesis, we will be able to read Genesis with much more understanding and with many fewer problems.

THE GOSPELS

It is of crucial importance for a Christian to know whether the Gospels are "true" or not. "If Christ has not been raised, your faith is futile and you are still in your sins" (1 Cor 15:17 RSV). It is also a matter of greatest importance to have a correct understanding of Christ's commands, for it is in the Gospels, more than in any other part of Scripture, that our faith in Christ is formed and our lives given direction.

Hence we can sometimes be bewildered when we first read the Gospels. We come to them expecting to find merely four "editions" of the life of Jesus. Since we believe they are faithful accounts of what Jesus did and said, we expect them to be in complete agreement with one another. It does not take us long, however, to discover that in many instances they are not in complete agreement, even when they are relating the same incident.

All four Gospels, for example, tell of Peter denying Christ three times. However, they differ from each other in describing who was questioning Peter. Matthew's rendition of the Lord's Prayer is significantly longer than Luke's; neither Mark nor John mention it. Matthew recounts nine beatitudes taught by Jesus; Luke has Jesus proclaiming four beatitudes and four curses; Mark and John omit all mention of beatitudes. If we were to judge by the Gospels of Matthew, Mark, and Luke, Jesus' public ministry lasted only one year; John's Gospel tells of a ministry that lasted over two years. The accounts of what happened on Easter morning vary with each Gospel.

Different approaches have been developed to explain the apparent discrepancies in the Gospel accounts. One method of interpretation maintains that the Gospels were the creation of the early Church and do not preserve any accurate records of Jesus. According to this approach, any attempt to know the life or words of the historical Jesus is doomed to failure. Quite often this approach to Scripture denies even the possibility that many of the incidents described in the Gospels could have happened; miracles are explained away as pious exaggerations, demon possession is dismissed as mental illness, and sometimes even the resurrection of Jesus is denied as wishful thinking on the part of the early Church.

A radically different and opposite approach maintains that every word of the Gospels is to be taken as literally true—the words Jesus speaks in the Gospels are the very words he spoke on earth. If apparent discrepancies exist, they can be accounted for in one way or another. In its extreme form, this approach insists on the literal interpretation of every word in the Gospels: the handling of poisonous snakes and the drinking of poison has been justified by Jesus' words in Mark 16:18.

Neither of these approaches is satisfactory for one who would read Scripture as the word of God addressed to us in human words. The first approach loses sight of the fact that Scripture is the word of God; the second approach fails to recognize that God's word is addressed to us in human words. To understand the Gospels correctly, we need to understand how and why they came to be written.

Three stages of development of the written Gospels can be identified. *First,* Jesus of Nazareth lived in our midst and taught. He relied on the spoken word, leaving behind him neither written works nor instructions to his followers to write his words down. Instead Jesus formed a small group of followers to be the nucleus of his Church. He consigned his teaching not to writing, but to this group of people. After his death and after the Holy Spirit had been poured out on the Church, this group proclaimed Jesus as the Lord. They taught what Jesus had taught them, and they also taught about Jesus.

This was the *second* stage of development of the Gospels: the teachings and life of the early Church. At least thirty years elapsed after the death of Jesus before the writing of the first Gospel that we have in the New Testament. During this time, the teaching of Jesus and the teaching about Jesus were handed on in the Church.

The needs of the Church influenced both the selection and presentation of the teachings of Jesus. What Jesus said about a specific topic was remembered in answer to questions and needs, and it was proclaimed in such a way as to answer these needs. The early Church was not concerned to report the words of Jesus or retell incidents from his life as a newspaper reporter might; it interpreted what Jesus did and said under the guidance of the Holy Spirit, highlighting its significance for our salvation.

Different kinds of needs influenced and shaped the handing on of the Gospels. There was first of all the need to preach the good news of Jesus Christ to those who had never heard it. The very basic outlines of Christ's life were proclaimed, as we see in the missionary sermons included in the Book of Acts: 2:22-36; 10:36-43; 13:23-39. The rough outline of these sermons became the rough outline for later writing of the Gospels: Jesus' public ministry of teaching and healing, beginning with his baptism at the hands of John; his death and resurrection, his present Lordship at the right hand of the Father. Miracles that Christ had worked were remembered and recounted as demonstrations of the arrival of God's kingdom. The needs of the listeners helped shape the way in which the miracle stories were proclaimed: a much greater emphasis was placed on the need to come to faith than on the miraculous event itself.

Another need of the early Church was to give further instructions for those who had already heard and accepted the Lordship of Jesus Christ. Many sayings of Jesus were remembered and taught to give direction on how to live the Christian life: the "Sermon on the Mount" is a good example of this. The needs of the listeners shaped the manner in which the words of Jesus were remembered and taught. It is doubtful that all of the sayings of Jesus that are preserved in Matthew's account of the Sermon on the Mount (chapters 5-7) were preached by Jesus on one occasion. Rather, various sayings of Jesus were compiled together to provide instruction on how a Christian lives.

Another need of the early Church was its common prayer life. The words of Jesus over the bread and wine during the Last Supper were remembered and used in liturgical contexts. Through constant repetition, they assumed a rather set form that was handed on as a part of the early Church's prayers.

The *third* stage of development of the written Gospels occurred when the evangelists set down the Gospels in writing. It should not be assumed that the evangelists merely wrote down an already completely developed oral tradition. The Gospel writers had a creative role to play—sifting various elements of the tradition, examining what others had already set down in writing, selecting some incidents and omitting others, giving order to the materials they selected. Their task was not a mechanical one, and they truly needed the inspiration of the Holy Spirit to carry it out.

On the other hand, the role of the Church in shaping the tradition that the evangelists drew from cannot be overlooked. The inspiration of the Spirit had to be present in the community as it shaped and handed on the good news about Jesus Christ. Mark and Luke were not eyewitnesses to the life of Jesus; they were entirely dependent on the remembrances of others.

We cannot, therefore, consider the Gospels to be stenographic records of the words Jesus spoke, set down in writing by the evangelists while the sound of his voice still echoed in the air. We cannot consider the Gospels to be biographies of Jesus Christ, as biographies are written today. Their purpose was not to provide a biographical account of a dead person, but to teach Christians about the one who still lived in their midst. Their purpose was to bring men and women to faith, and to nurture them as they grew in that faith. Incidents from the life of Jesus that had no bearing on this purpose were omitted—although it would be an astonishing oversight for a biography to be silent about so many years of the life of Christ, and to give no physical description of him whatsoever. The Gospels were not written to satisfy the merely curious.

The early Church was much less concerned to preserve the

exact words of Jesus than it was to preserve and proclaim their significance. It may shock many Christians today to realize that the Gospels do not necessarily contain the "exact words" Jesus Christ spoke. They definitely contain the message that Jesus proclaimed, but the wording was shaped by the early Church to highlight Jesus' meaning. Hence the apparent discrepancies in the wording between the Gospels—something unexplainable if the Gospels were transcripts of Jesus' speeches. The early Church did not have tape recorders and on-site stenographers; it did have the Holy Spirit to guarantee its faithfulness to what Jesus taught. Words were only a means of making the Word present. The focus of the Church was not on what Christ said in the past, but on what he was continuing to say in its midst.

The fact that our Gospels do not necessarily contain the "exact words" of Jesus does not mean that they do not contain the words of Jesus to us. The inspiration of the Spirit kept the Church faithful to what Jesus taught as it handed on his message, and it kept the evangelists faithful to what Jesus taught as they compiled and set down that tradition in writing. There are instances where we can be fairly sure that the Church did preserve his exact words—for instance, his referring to God as "Abba," Father.

We should also remember that today we must depend on translations to convey the message of Jesus to us. In order to go from one language to another, a translator must inevitably make interpretations in order to be faithful to the thought and meaning of the original, as well as its words. Jesus spoke and taught in Aramaic. The Gospels were written in Greek—the most common language of the Church at the time they were written. They were hence a translation of what Jesus taught from their very beginning. In only a very few instances did the Gospel writers preserve any Aramaic words—"Abba" being one of them. The Bibles we read today are translations from the Greek, involving another step of interpretation.

All this is not to say that the Gospels were simply an invention of the early Church that put words in the mouth of Jesus and made up incidents to suit the Church's needs. To shape a teaching to fit a particular need is not the same as making up a teaching. To dwell on the significance of an event requires that the event itself has occurred. If nothing had really happened, then there would have been no good news.

Those who claim that we cannot discover what Jesus was like or taught overlook the basis of the Gospels, the first stage of their development, the words and actions of Jesus himself. They overlook the fact that Jesus commissioned the apostles to be his "witnesses" (Acts 1:8). In a courtroom, a "witness" is someone who has firsthand acquaintance with a piece of evidence. The apostles were commissioned to be Christ's "witnesses" precisely because they had seen him with their own eyes and heard him with their ears. This firsthand acquaintance was a requirement for the replacement selected for Judas (Acts 1:21-22).

The Gospels grew out of the testimony of these firsthand witnesses. John's first letter was written about a reality "that we have heard, and we have seen with our own eyes; that we have watched and touched with our hands: the Word, who is life" (1 Jn 1:1 JB). His Gospel preserves this intimate firsthand acquaintance, even if one of John's disciples did the final editing, for John "is the one who vouches for these things and has written them down, and we know that his testimony is true" (Jn 21:24 JB). Luke tried to set down in writing the good news of Jesus Christ as "events that have taken place among us, exactly as these were handed down to us by those who from the outset were eyewitnesses and ministers of the word" (Lk 1:2 JB).

On the other hand, those who go to lengths to reconcile the variations between the four Gospels tend to overlook the second stage of their development: the handing on of the faith within the Church between the ascension of Christ and the setting down in writing of the Gospels we read today. The Gospels were a proclamation of the early Church, a proclamation that the same Jesus who had walked in their midst was the Lord. They were a proclamation formed by the needs of the Church.

The Church has continually and strongly affirmed the historical character of the Gospels. The Church has firmly believed that the Gospels faithfully hand on what Jesus Christ did and taught for our salvation. The application of the gospel message to particular situations in the early Church did not do away with its historical basis in the life of Jesus. The shaping of the gospel message by its oral handing on did not do away with its historical roots. The work of the evangelists in writing the Gospels—selecting some incidents and omitting others, combining together teachings given on different occasions, explaining the significance of what Christ did in terms of the needs of the early Church—did not do violence to the truth of the gospel message. The eyewitnesses and evangelists wanted to tell the truth about Jesus Christ. Through the inspiration of the Holy Spirit, they did. With that certainty we can read the Gospels not as journalists' accounts, but as proclamations of the salvation to be found in Jesus Christ. We can truly read the words of Jesus in the Gospels as his words to us.

THE BOOK OF REVELATION

When we turn to the Book of Revelation, we encounter probably the most difficult book of the Bible to understand—one that has given rise to more current misunderstandings than any other book.

The reason for our perplexity is obvious: the Book of Revelation teems with symbols—monsters, mysterious numbers, obscure allusions—all wrapped up in visions which the author, John, has received. Because of its inherent obscurity, and because it purports to be a revelation of things to come, the Book of Revelation has received an amazing variety of interpretations. Some claim that it predicts the creation of the European Common Market, the invention of helicopters, the horrors of H-bombs, and the imminent end of the world.

An understanding of literary form is nowhere more important than in the Book of Revelation. The Greek title of this book is the "Apocalypse of John," identifying the book as an apocalypse. Unfortunately, the apocalyptic form of writing is to modern minds the least familiar of the Bible's various literary forms, and hence the most misunderstood.

Apocalyptic writing began toward the end of the age of prophecy in Old Testament times. Some of the prophetic books of the Old Testament exhibit apocalyptic elements, notably the Books of Daniel, Ezekiel, and Zechariah. Apocalyptic writings became very common in the second and first centuries B.C., and continued to be written for about a century after Christ. The only apocalyptic book preserved in the New Testament is the Apocalypse of John.

Apocalyptic writings claimed to be revelations of events to come. The revelation was usually given in a vision. The revelations contained in apocalyptic writings were expressed through symbols; to understand the revelation, one had to understand the symbols being employed.

Few if any of the symbols used in the Apocalypse of John are symbols familiar to us today. Hence readers of the Apocalypse need a key to interpret what is being said. And since virtually everything mentioned in an apocalyptic writing has a symbolic value, the Book of Revelation will be almost totally incomprehensible without an understanding of the symbolism being employed. Just as Americans cannot understand the highly developed symbolism of Japanese theater without an explanation, and just as a Tibetan peasant would be totally mystified at seeing his first baseball game, so a modern reader cannot comprehend the world of apocalyptic writing without guidance.

The most important factor in understanding the Book of Revelation is to realize that it was a tract for its times. It was written in a specific context, and addressed itself to a concrete situation. It was written toward the end of the first century, when the Church was undergoing persecution at the hands of Roman emperors. It was written to encourage Christians in the midst of this persecution. Unless this primary focus of the book is kept in mind, no accurate understanding of it is possible.

Part of the difficulty in understanding the Book of Revelation lies in the fact that it doesn't appear to be a tract for Christians undergoing Roman persecution at the end of the first century. It appears to be prophecy about the end of the world, describing battle between God and Satan, proclaiming the ultimate triumph of God in the midst of terrible suffering on earth. There is a sense in which these matters are dealt with in the Book of Revelation, but they are dealt with in the context of events at the end of the first century. Simply put, John was not writing to twentieth-century Americans; he was writing to first-century Christians in Asia Minor. If we read Revelations as if it were written to describe events in the twentieth century, or as if it were written to predict events that are just around the corner for us, we misread it. We must read it first of all as a message written to first-century Christians in a time of persecution.

The message that John wished to convey was one of encouragement and hope. He wished to console Christians in their sufferings and to assure them that their sufferings were not overlooked in God's plan. He wished to assure them that God was still with them, and that God was still the Lord of history despite Rome's apparent domination. He wished to teach that God will judge both the just and the unjust, and that those who have turned to Christ will be rewarded in the afterlife. God's work of redemption was not yet complete; Christians were not to despair in the midst of suffering and death at the hands of Rome.

John expressed this message in apocalyptic terms. The persecution waged by Rome against Christians was seen as an assault of Satan on God himself—an assault that God would overcome. Satan would be cast into a fiery pit: Rome would be destroyed. Martyrs would be welcomed in heaven by Christ himself, whose sufferings they participated in: they were those who had washed their robes in the blood of the Lamb.

The important point is that the symbolism of the Book of Revelation must be interpreted in terms of the intent of the author and the situation that he addressed when he wrote. There is a timeless message to the Book of Revelation: it is God's word to us. But we must first of all understand it in terms of its message to the Church in a time of persecution. If we understand what it said then, we will have taken the first step to understanding what it may say to us now. We cannot directly interpret its symbols in terms of current events. We cannot interpret its mention of a thousand-year reign of Christ as a literal prediction that Christ will live again on earth for one thousand years and reign over the kingdoms of the earth. We cannot take its descriptions of calamities as descriptions of events that are happening now (and happening now for the first time since John wrote), and from that deduce that the end of the world is at hand. We cannot predict the political and military fortunes of the modern state of Israel on the basis of what is contained in the Book of Revelation.

An introduction to the Book of Revelation, such as that found in the full editions of the Jerusalem Bible, is a necessity for the modern reader. Also necessary is an almost line-by-line commentary that explains the significance that the symbols used in Revelation has for first-century readers. *The Apocalypse* by Fr. George Montague, S.M., can be recommended for its sound judgment (Servant Publications, 1992).

THE SILENCE OF THE SCRIPTURES

We have seen three areas in which sacred Scripture does not intend to teach us about things we might like to know. The Bible does not give us a scientific account of the creation of the universe; it reveals that all that exists comes from the hand of God, but doesn't duplicate the work of the scientist. The Gospels are not a biography of the life of Jesus Christ; they are proclamations of the saving truth that Jesus of Nazareth is the Son of God, and that through him we find salvation. The Book of Revelation does not describe how or when the world will end; it only assures us of the ultimate triumph and coming of the kingdom of God.

The Bible is not a textbook, and even less is it a book of texts. We cannot demand information from it that it does not contain. We cannot demand answers to questions that it does not address. We cannot use it as we would a cookbook or an encyclopedia or a book of amazing facts. We cannot make the Bible out to be something different than it is.

The Bible is the word of God to us and for us. It is God's revelation of himself, and of our way to the Father. It is the

Church's rule of faith. But the Bible is not a book of instructions dropped from the heavens as a complete guide to our every decision and a total answer to our every question. The Bible cannot replace the Church as the context in which we live our Christian lives and encounter Christ, even if it is an important part of that context. The Bible cannot replace the guidance of the Holy Spirit as we wrestle with problems and questions unique to our modern age.

The Bible is silent on many points. It tells us little about life after death. Had we been in Bethany at the time, we would almost certainly have asked Lazarus what it was like to be dead for three days. Yet John is silent about this; the point he wishes to make is the power of Jesus over life and death, not the nature of Lazarus' experience while dead.

The Bible promises us a resurrection of our bodies, but does not describe what our resurrected bodies will look like or feel like. We would naturally like to know. But Paul dismisses the question quite brusquely: "Someone may ask, 'How are dead people raised, and what sort of body do they have when they come back?' They are stupid questions. Whatever you sow in the ground has to die before it is given new life and the thing that you sow is not what is going to come.... It is the same with the resurrection of the dead: the thing that is sown is perishable but what is raised is imperishable" (1 Cor 15:35-37, 42 JB). Beyond Paul's analogy, the Scripture keeps silent.

The questions we ask of Scripture can be the wrong questions. We could ask, "How did the world really begin?" or "How will the world end?" and expect to find answers in the first and last books of the Bible. But Genesis and Revelation were not written to answer those questions, and answers cannot legitimately be extracted from them. Probably more bad interpretation of Scripture has been "based" on these two books than the rest of the Bible put together—largely because the wrong kinds of questions were being asked.

We would like to know the time when Christ will come again in glory. Like the apostles, we would ask, "Lord, has the time come? Are you going to restore the kingdom?" (Acts 1:6 JB).

But his answer to us is the same as his answer to them: "It is not for you to know times or dates that the Father has decided by his own authority, but you will receive power when the Holy Spirit comes on you, and then you will be my witnesses" (Acts 1:7-8 JB). It is not for us to know... but a task has been set before us. We are to receive the power of the Holy Spirit and get on with the work of being God's children in the world today, and not idly speculate about more than has been revealed to us.

The promise we have received is a promise of a full knowledge of God. But it is a promise that God will fulfill hereafter, not here and now through the words of the Bible. We can apply Paul's words to Scripture itself: "Now we are seeing a dim reflection in a mirror; but then we shall be seeing face to face. The knowledge that I have now is imperfect; but then I shall know as fully as I am known" (1 Cor 13:12 JB). The word of God is a mirror in which we see him and see ourselves. When we have completed our journey to the Father, we shall see him face-to-face, we shall know him even as he now knows us. We shall not only hear the word of God addressed to us; we will be completely in the presence of the Word of God.

Until that day when we see him face-to-face, we are privileged to see him as he has revealed himself to us. We are privileged to be able to listen to his words to us. We are privileged to have Scripture, and to be able to read it as the word of God, revealing God himself to us, inviting us along on that path that leads into his presence.

The Power of the Word

T HE WORD OF GOD that we read in Scripture is no ordinary
word. It is a word with power, a word with the power to
change us. If we read the Bible correctly we should experience
something of the power of the word as we read. We should
come into contact with God who speaks to us, and that contact
should change us.

The world around us is full of words. Few of them have much
impact on us. We swim through the day in a sea of words—
words spoken to us, words we read in newspapers and magazines, words from the TV set, words from a radio blaring
somewhere in the background. We have learned to ignore most
of these words; we have become good at listening without hearing. Even when we want to hear words addressed to us, we
sometimes find that we have lost the ability to pay attention.
How many times have we had to ask someone to repeat what
they said because our mind had wandered and we didn't hear
what they were saying to us? How many times have we come
home from church on Sunday and when asked what the sermon
was about could not remember?

Most of the words we hear are of only passing interest, if of
any interest at all to us. They are disposable words, sentences
written or uttered once and then forgotten. We use yesterday's
sports pages to wrap our garbage. Perhaps forty thousand books
are published in the United States each year; most of them will
not be around very long. Almost half of the paperback books

printed will never be purchased but will be fed unread into a paper shredder to be recycled into yet other unread books.

It is all too easy to miss God's word in this deluge of words. It is all too easy to read the Bible as if it were a book like any other book. It is almost natural to put God's words on a par with the other words we read and hear each day, and for God's words to be lost in the babble.

But God assures us that his word is unlike any other word. It may be spoken to us in our everyday language; it may be printed with the same kind of type on the same kind of paper that we use to print other words. But the word of God is different. It has a power that no other words have. It has an ability to affect our lives as no other words do. It addresses us with an authority that no other words can claim.

The word of God is not magical. It is a word that has power because of the one who speaks it. The authority of the word of God rests on the authority of God; the ability of the word of God to change us stems from God's desire to save us. Just as our words can be a bridge from one human to another, the word of God is a bridge between God and us.

To appreciate the nature and power of the word of God, let us imagine when there was all silence. Let us imagine that time before time when there were no voices, no words, no things. Into this absolute void the first words were spoken; they were God's words, words of creation. "God said, 'Let there be light'; and there was light" (Gn 1:3 JB). God said, let creation come forth from nothing, and creation came forth. God said, let the sounds of birds and animals and all kinds of living creatures fill the earth, and at his word the sounds of nature began. "God said, 'Let us make man in our image'" (Gn 1:26 JB), and at the word of God human words began to be spoken and heard. God's voice sounded through nothingness, and his word brought forth all that is.

By the word of Yahweh the heavens were made,
Their whole array by the breath of his mouth;
he collects the ocean waters as though in a wineskin,
he stores the deeps in cellars.

Let the whole world fear Yahweh,
let all who live on earth revere him!
He spoke, and it was created;
he commanded and there it stood.   **Psalm 33:6-9 JB**

The word of God is not a disposable word, but a word that lasts forever. The word of God uttered at creation still echoes throughout the vastness of the universe, holding it in being. The word of God spoken to the first man and woman is valid still for every man and woman. "The grass withers, the flower fades, but the word of our God remains for ever" (Is 40:8 JB).

This word of God that called forth creation from nothing, this word of God that lasts forever, is addressed to individual men and women. God calls each of his creatures by name. His word summons them from nothing, and his word addresses them as his creatures and his children. The word of God is not only a cosmic word, but a personal word.

He gives an order;
his word flashes to earth:
to spread snow like a blanket,
to strew hoarfrost like ashes,

to drop ice like breadcrumbs,
and when the cold is unbearable,
he sends his word to bring the thaw
and warm wind to melt the snow.

He reveals his word to Jacob,
his statutes and rulings to Israel:
he never does this for other nations,
he never reveals his rulings to them.   **Psalm 147:15-20**

God spoke his word to Abraham and Isaac and Jacob, and to their descendants, his people. God spoke his word to Moses and the prophets, and through them to every member of the chosen people. God spoke his word finally by sending the Word to become flesh, so that all men might hear the word of God and find everlasting life.

The word that God speaks is not a superficial word, a word that only grazes the surface. It is rather a word that speaks to our innermost being, a word that knows the secrets of our hearts and reveals them to us. "For the word of God is living and active, sharper than any two-edged sword, piercing to the division of soul and spirit, of joints and marrow, and discerning the thoughts and intentions of the heart. And before him no creature is hidden, but all are open and laid bare to the eyes of him with whom we have to do" (Heb 4:12-13 RSV). The word of God is more personal than any other word we will ever hear. Nothing of our individual uniqueness is hidden from God, and nothing in us can ever be shielded from his word. We are transparent to the eyes of God and the word of God.

The word of God is also an effective word. So many of the words we speak in a day seem to have no impact; they are words merely to pass the time of day. Even those words that we intend to have an impact often fall short of our intention. But God's words are not idle; God does not speak to amuse himself. What God speaks he intends, and what he intends he brings to pass. God assured Jeremiah, "I too watch over my word to see it fulfilled" (Jer 1:12 JB). Every word from God's mouth is an eternally valid and powerful word, a word that demands its fulfillment. "Yes, as the rain and the snow come down from the heavens and do not return without watering the earth, making it yield and giving growth to provide seed for the sower and bread for the eating, so the word that goes from my mouth does not return to me empty, without carrying out my will and succeeding in what it was sent to do" (Is 55:10-11 JB).

What is the word of God sent to do? God's word is basically a creative word. God's word brought forth creation, and now God's word brings forth his new creation. God's word created people for himself, and now God's word creates a new chosen people for himself. God's word called us from nothingness into life, and now God's word calls us to new life in Jesus Christ. "Your new birth was not from any mortal seed but from the everlasting word of the living and eternal God" (1 Pt 1:23 JB). The word of God is addressed to us to make us a part of his new creation. God's purpose in speaking to us is to bring us to eternal life.

God does not want his word to us to be in vain. He speaks to each of us as individuals and watches over his word to us to see that it is heard and obeyed. He sends his word to us not to have it echo emptily back to him but to have it carry out his will in our lives. He sends his word to us to bring us to himself, as an abundant harvest.

We must so read God's word. We must honor it as his word, as a word unlike any other word. We must welcome his word into our hearts as we welcome no other word. We must bend our wills to his word in obedience. We must allow his word to change us, to remold our lives into the lives he wants us to live. God told Jeremiah that he was putting his word into his mouth, so that Jeremiah could tear down and build up, could overthrow and plant (Jer 1:9-10). The word of God would similarly tear down whatever within us needs tearing down and build up that which needs building up. The word of God to us would overthrow sin and false values in our lives and plant the seed of eternal life.

The word of God was sent to the Israelites in a variety of ways. God spoke to them and led them through the leaders he had appointed, such as Moses. God guided them through his written laws. God spoke particular words to them through the prophets. So too the word of God comes to us in a variety of ways. It comes through the leaders God has appointed for his Church. It comes through the written word in Scripture and the teachings of the Church. It comes even today in prophetic words. It comes through personal words to us in prayer. It is folly to try to play off one form of God's speaking to us against another form: it is the same God who speaks, and we should be eager to hear him through whatever channel he would address us.

Our reading of the word of God in Scripture is one privileged access we have to the word of God. We should read and revere the Bible as God's word to us, as a book unlike any other book. We should turn to it with eagerness each day, because our creator and redeemer stands ready to speak to us through its words.

If we are reading the Bible properly, we should experience

something of the power of God's word as we read. This does not mean that we should expect to experience a spiritual high every time we open our Bible. But it means that we should have some conviction that what we read is God's word to us, and we should find it making a difference in our lives. There may be times when we do indeed feel as if the word we read in Scripture was a word addressed to us alone, a word that is indeed a razor-sharp sword piercing through to the innermost depths of our hearts. There may be less dramatic times, when we simply nod assent that what we read is indeed God's truth for us, and that our lives must change accordingly.

We should not set out to have spiritual ecstasies when we read Scripture. We should rather set out to read it as God's word: to read it with attention, with submission, as the word of him who created us. We should hope for its power to be released in our lives. The fruit we should expect from our reading should be the fruit of the Spirit, especially self-sacrificing love, and the joy of being personally addressed by God.

We should not read God's word as being a word of condemnation for us. It is a word that would guide and correct us, but it is first of all a word of love and a word of life. The first truth that God would reveal to us is that he loves us. This is a truth that he would speak to us day after day because it is a truth that we seem to forget that often. God's word to us is a word that is meant to call us forth to life. If God had wanted to condemn us, he could have done so in silence. His very speaking to us is evidence of his love for us and his desire that we have eternal life.

God's words in Scripture assuring us of his love for us lend themselves well to our reading them as God's personal word to us and experiencing their power in our life. If we read those passages of the Bible that reveal God's love as being personally addressed to us we should experience their impact on our lives. If we ponder and reflect on God's words of love to us, we should be changed by them. God tells us of his love so that we might have life.

Conclusion

And now I commend you to God, and to the word of his grace that has the power to build you up and to give you your inheritance among all the sanctified. Acts 20:32 JB

OF ALL CITIES in which Paul proclaimed the good news of salvation, none was more dear to his heart than Ephesus. It was Paul who brought the full message of Christianity to Ephesus, teaching about the role of the Holy Spirit (Acts 19:1-7). According to Acts 20:31, Paul stayed at Ephesus for three years—longer than at any other city along his missionary route.

After his extended stay in Ephesus, Paul spent some months in Greece, and then journeyed back toward Ephesus. Paul was anxious to get to Jerusalem in time to celebrate Pentecost, and so did not go into Ephesus itself. Instead he stopped at the nearby seaport town of Miletus and sent for the elders of the Church at Ephesus to visit him there. They were his dear friends, his converts, his co-workers, and he wanted to say goodbye to them before continuing on to Jerusalem.

Paul's farewell was an especially heartfelt one. The Holy Spirit had revealed that persecution and imprisonment lay before him. Paul told his Ephesian friends, "I now feel sure that none of you among whom I have gone about proclaiming the kingdom will ever see my face again" (Acts 20:25 JB). After Paul addressed words of farewell, "he knelt down with them all and prayed. By now they were in tears; they put their arms around Paul's neck and kissed him; what saddened them most was his saying they would never see his face again. Then they escorted him to the ship" (Acts 20:36-38 JB).

Understood in this setting, Paul's final exhortation to the Ephesians takes on special significance. Paul was not merely giving out good general advice; Paul was addressing last words of instruction to close friends, those now responsible for guiding the Church at Ephesus. The moment was a solemn one, not to be wasted.

Paul exhorted the elders to watch over the Church at Ephesus with diligence, reminding them of his own example. And then he gave them a final solemn word of exhortation and encouragement: "And now I commend you to God, and to the word of his grace that has the power to build you up and to give you your inheritance among all the sanctified" (Acts 20:32 JB).

The "word of his grace" that Paul referred to was the message of salvation that he had handed on to them, the message that was even then being put into writing as the books of the New Testament. The word of grace was the good news of who Jesus Christ is and what he has done for us. The word of grace was the message through which we too find salvation, the message that releases the power of God in our midst, giving us our inheritance among all the children of God.

If Paul were to address a farewell message to us, it would likely be the same message. He would commend us into the hands of God, reminding us of the loving care the Father has for us. He would remind us that true life comes to us through Jesus Christ, God's provision for our eternal salvation. He would exhort us to be filled with the Holy Spirit and to live out our lives as sons and daughters of God. And Paul would exhort us to draw daily strength from the message of salvation that we have heard, from the good news that has been handed on to us, from the word of God that has been addressed to us. He would remind us that the word of God in Scripture is a word of grace and power, a word leading to salvation.

The word of God spoken to us through the words of Scripture has the power to build us up, to equip us to live out the

Christian life, to encourage and direct us. The word of God is a guiding word, a strengthening word, an encouraging word, leading us on to the place of our inheritance.

Our part must be to be faithful to the word of God. We must be faithful in reading it in Scripture; we must be faithful in our obedience to it. God will be faithful to us, speaking to us, fulfilling the promises he has made to us, drawing us along the path to himself.

A Postscript—1998
Reading Scripture
After Thirty-Four Years

PRESUMABLY AGE BRINGS WISDOM along with thinning hair. What have I learned about reading the Bible after having been at it for thirty-four years? There are a few things I might say.

I began to read Scripture on Ash Wednesday, 1964. I had dipped into the Bible before but never read it in a serious or sustained way. As a result of making a Cursillo (a weekend "short course in Christianity"), I resolved to read Scripture every day during Lent. It was a modest enough commitment: fifteen minutes of Scripture reading and reflection after my breakfast coffee had taken effect. When Lent was over, I kept on reading. And by the grace of God, I read Scripture to discover what it said as God's word to me. Even though I enjoyed studying (I was in graduate school at the time), I did not set out to read the Bible to study it but to hear God's word to me and to respond to him in prayer.

I realize now what a great grace from God this was, getting me off on the right foot. I still try to read Scripture or listen to it proclaimed in the Liturgy in the same way I did thirty-four years ago: as God's word to me. This doesn't mean I always succeed (distractions are ever-beckoning fields in which my mind is eager to frolic), but my aim is to open myself to God's word whenever I read the Bible or hear its words proclaimed.

I do not want to downplay the importance of studying the Bible and making use of the work of scholars. Study is very important, but it is only the first step. Much of my time over the last two decades was spent studying the Bible in order to write about it. This involved consulting commentaries and even wrestling in a limited way with the original Hebrew and Greek texts. But when I finished my homework with the commentaries, I set them aside and said to myself, "OK— granted all that the scholars say—what does this text of Scripture mean as God's word to me?"

Commentaries and other study aids are of help in understanding what the words of Scripture meant when they were written. But what is their meaning today, to me, to those for whom I write? That is the key question I pose to myself when I read Scripture, both for my own spiritual nourishment and as a part of my writing. I think it is the key question every Christian should ask as he or she reads the Bible.

Yet even if reading for personal meaning has been a constant for me through the decades, there have been some changes in how I read Scripture.

My reflecting on Scripture is less programmed than when I first began. Then I had a fixed time each day for reading and reflecting. Now I find myself pondering the words of Scripture periodically throughout the day. One of the Scripture readings during morning Mass may trigger reflections that continue after Mass is over. A phrase or line from a hymn may echo a verse of Scripture, drawing my mind to the passage. A situation I encounter during the day may bring a scriptural parallel to mind. Or sometimes a particular passage will just pop into my mind unexpectedly, bearing a meaning or application that I had never before noted. Some of this began to happen rather soon after I began regular Scripture reading, but it has become an even more common experience for me in recent years.

I do not want to give the impression that my mind is constantly taken up with God or Scripture, for it surely is not. But the cumulative effect of years of reading Scripture is that a good deal of biblical material has entered my memory banks, and it periodically pushes its way into my consciousness, distracting me from my chronic distractions, drawing my mind to God.

Another by-product of thirty-four years of Scripture reading is that I know more of the context of particular biblical passages. For example, if a selection from one of the prophets is read during Mass, many times I can recall the historical setting in which that prophecy was uttered. This helps me appreciate something of the significance the prophecy had for those to whom it was first addressed, and this in turn often suggests an application of the prophetic message for today. Because of my years of reading the Bible, I am now better able to understand Scripture contextually—a dimension of its meaning I often missed when I first began to read the Bible.

My first years of reading Scripture were filled with the excitement of new discovery. I had never encountered most of the books of the Bible, much less taken their words to heart. When I began to read the Bible, I had the expectation that I would discover something new and living and transforming every day. By the grace of the Holy Spirit, I usually did.

After thirty-four years, much of that excitement has worn off—but not the sense of newness. I am amazed that I still discover new insights each time I read the Gospels, even though I have, through the years, read them many times and studied them with the help of a fair number of commentaries. The Bible is no longer new to me in the sense of novelty but new in the sense of always containing new depths of meaning that await my discovery.

The ever-newness of Scripture is partly a characteristic of Scripture and partly a grace God gives us as we read it. St. Augustine wrote, "For such is the depth of the Christian Scriptures that, even if I were attempting to study them and nothing else, from boyhood to decrepit old age, with the utmost leisure, the most unwearied zeal, and with talents greater than I possess, I would still be making progress in discovering their treasures." I think God gives most everyone who perseveres in reading Scripture over a number of years a sense of what Augustine describes.

If I do not always find reading Scripture as exciting as I remember it being three decades ago, neither is my marriage as exciting as it was in the days when my wife Mary and I faced life with the energy and ideals of newlyweds. But that does not mean that our marriage has gone downhill. Our love has deepened and matured through the years; I now love and appreciate Mary more than I did when we were first married.

Growth in marriage is a good analogy for growth in reading Scripture, for both are a matter of a relationship. Reading Scripture is a facet of our relationship with God and cannot be understood apart from it. Has my relationship with God changed in the last thirty-four years? Of course. So it should be no surprise that my reading of the Bible as his word has changed as well.

The great spiritual writers of the Church have insisted that growth in holiness is not a matter of achieving ever higher spiritual highs. So too growth in reading Scripture cannot be a matter of attaining ever bigger spiritual goosebumps as we read. If God chooses to motivate us by such means, fine; but they are not the reason we read his word, and their absence does not mean that he is no longer speaking to us.

Growth in reading Scripture should be growth in our understanding of its inspired meaning but also growth in taking it to heart. I know I have grown in my understanding of the books of the Bible over the last thirty-four years; growth in taking it to heart is harder to measure. The difficulty is one of measuring growth in our relationship with God. Feeling holier doesn't mean being holier: the Pharisee praying in the temple in Jesus' parable certainly felt holy (see Luke 18:9-14).

I wish I could say that I am much more eager to repent of sin and embrace God's will now than I was three decades ago, but I am not so sure that I really am. Then as now I only move toward God under the impulse of his grace. Did God give me more grace back in the days of my initial zeal and first love, or is he giving me more now when I can see my ingrained sins more clearly? I don't know: I don't have a scale to measure God's grace.

And that means, ultimately, I don't have a scale for measuring growth in reading Scripture as God's word, or measuring growth in listening to God. I don't even try to make such measurement of my Scripture reading: I simply try to stay faithful to reading Scripture and listening for God's word, and leave it to him to judge whether I am doing a better or worse job of it year by year.

I hope these reflections encourage you to stick with reading Scripture, in season and out of season, whether you think you are treading water or think you are making progress. Don't try to measure the impact of God's word on your life by counting spiritual goosebumps. Don't expect that God will speak to you the same way through Scripture today as he did five or ten or twenty-five or fifty years ago. Learn as much about the Bible as you can, and then go before God, alone with his word, and listen to what he has to say to you. Don't demand he speak with thunder and lightning when he is trying to talk to you in a still small voice. Don't mistake his silence for his not speaking. Don't stop reading; don't stop listening. Abide in his word, as in a marriage that will never end.

I pray that God will give me the grace to do just that: abide in his word, until in eternity he speaks to me face-to-face.

George Martin
Ash Wednesday, 1998

Introduction to Study Guide

I BEGAN WRITING *Reading Scripture as the Word of God* twenty-five years ago, after having been convinced for some time that such a book was needed. I had previously worked in Catholic adult education, organizing Scripture classes along with other programs. Finding good textbooks for Scripture courses was a challenge, for there were not nearly as many good books out on the Bible back then as there are now. Those that were available shared a shortcoming: while they might have explained the Bible, they did not explain how one ought to go about *reading* the Bible.

Yet that was the help most of the adults who enrolled in Scripture courses needed. Like many Catholics, they had grown up not reading the Bible. Now, in the wake of the Second Vatican Council, they wanted to start. And yet, they didn't know exactly where to begin: *What translation should I use? How should I apply the message of the Bible to my life today? What do I do when I come across a passage I do not understand?* Introductions to Scripture and commentaries on its books did not address such questions.

I had started reading Scripture on a daily basis some years earlier, and through trial and error discovered a workable program for myself. I had also come across a sermon by Soren Kierkegaard, a nineteenth-century Danish Lutheran, that contained some valuable pointers for reading Scripture as God's word addressed to us. His ideas were of great help to me, and my wife lovingly and laboriously typed out Kierkegaard's sermon on mimeograph stencils so that I could make copies for my friends. (This happened in the Dark Ages, before instant copy services were ever established. If our children were faced with the same need today, they would probably post

Kierkegaard's sermon on a Web site and notify their friends by E-mail of its availability.)

Alas, Mary's efforts were to little avail. Many of my friends had difficulty coping with Kierkegaard's manner of expression, and had a hard time profiting from his insights. I resolved to make a simplified paraphrase of Kierkegaard's sermon someday, to help others benefit from his thoughts.

That someday never came. Instead, with my adult education experience behind me, I sat down to attempt the more ambitious project of writing a "do it yourself" manual for reading Scripture as God's word to us. I incorporated not only Kierkegaard's insights but those of others, filtered through my own experience in reading the Bible. The book that resulted, *Reading Scripture as the Word of God*, has helped a number of people get off on the right foot in reading the Bible, if I may judge from the letters and comments I have received.

This study guide edition is designed to assist readers and groups in making use of the book. The questions will help individuals to get a clearer understanding of not only why to read Scripture but how to profit from reading Scripture as God's word. For groups, these same questions should provide a basis for sharing experiences and insights, in order to help each other read Scripture as God's word.

Some study guides pose questions whose answers are found in the text of the book. The questions in this study guide are of a different sort. Often the questions focus on how you, the reader, make use of the information and suggestions found in the book. Sometimes the questions will call for your own reflections on a topic covered in the book. In short, the study guide invites your response to what you read, rather than a simple repetition of what you read.

For both individuals and groups, I recommend beginning to read the Bible itself right from the start, rather than waiting until one finishes reading this book. This will give the questions in the study guide a practical relevance and application. Members of a group could decide to read the same book of the Bible in order to focus their sharing. Alternatively, it could be left up to each member of the group to decide where to begin reading, so that a greater variety of experiences can be shared.

I must thank Servant Publications' editorial director (and my best friend), Bert Ghezzi, for his continuing enthusiasm for *Reading Scripture as the Word of God*. I did not think to include a dedication in the book when I wrote it, but this edition gives me the opportunity to dedicate it to Bert. I also want to thank my wife Mary, who typed those mimeograph stencils so many years ago, and who was lovingly patient as I spent my free hours writing, leaving her with the practical burdens of caring for our five children.

George Martin

Study Guide

Preface
The Purpose of This Book

1. What do I hope to get out of this book? *(7-8)*

Part I: Reading Scripture

Chapter One
Reading

In summary: Beginning to read the Bible.

1. Why am I interested in reading the Bible? What is drawing me to Scripture? *(11-12)*

2. Have I ever experienced God speaking his word to me? How? *("Daily Reading," 12-15)*

3. How often do I read the Bible now? Every day? Most every day? Once a week? Occasionally? Rarely?

4. Can I commit myself to daily reading at a set time each day, at least for a trial period of one month?

5. Do I tend to read Scripture in big chunks? Or do I usually read a few verses at a time and meditate on them? Or do I do something in between? How well does my approach work for me? *("Kinds of Reading," 15-17)*

6. What time each day for reading the Bible will work best for me? *("Some Practical Considerations," 18-25)*

7. What translation(s) of the Bible do I own? What translation(s) do I use most often? Am I satisfied with it (them)?

8. What words would I use to ask the Holy Spirit to help me as I read Scripture? *("Prayer Before Reading," 25-26)*

Editor's note: The italicized numbers in parentheses correspond to the pages of the text relevant to that question and those that follow, up to the next italicized citation.

9. What is my track record at keeping my resolutions? Am I committed to making a sustained effort to read Scripture every day? (*"Faithfulness and Humility,"* 27-30)

In conclusion: You are at the starting line. Ready, get set, go!

Chapter Two
Understanding

In summary: Understanding the Bible is worth our thought and effort.

1. Is the biblical world a foreign land for me, or do I feel at home in it? (*31-33*)

2. Do I dread having to study, or do I enjoy learning new things? What was my last experience of acquiring a new skill—learning how to do something I did not know how to do before? (*"Why Study?"* 33-37)

3. Does the prospect of studying the Bible appeal to me, or is it simply one more duty competing for my time? Am I personally convinced that reading the Bible as God's word demands some study?

4. The Second Vatican Council taught that "all that the inspired authors [of Scripture] affirm should be regarded as affirmed by the Holy Spirit" (Divine Revelation, #11). Therefore we should "carefully search out the meaning that the sacred authors really had in mind—the meaning that God wanted to manifest by means of their words" (#12). When I read the Bible, do I try to grasp the meaning that the inspired authors of Scripture intended their words to have? How might I more sharply focus on that meaning? (*"Some Principles of Study,"* 37-41)

5. Some of the types of writing (or "literary forms") used in the Bible are prayers, parables, letters, and history. What other types of writing have I found in the Bible?

6. What book of the Bible am I now reading or am I about to read? What simple steps might I take to enrich my reading by a little study of this biblical book? (*"Practical Approaches to Study,"* 41-45)

7. Can I think of an example of how examining the context of a particular Scripture passage helped me better understand it?

8. What study aids are included in the edition of the Bible that I read? Which of these study aids do I make use of when I read Scripture? (*"Using Study Aids,"* 45-51)

9. What other Scripture study aids do I have at my disposal? Which of them have I found helpful? What kind of help did they give me? What other study aid might help me better understand Scripture?

In conclusion: A little extra effort can reap a bountiful harvest of understanding.

Chapter Three
Listening

In summary: God wants to speak to us; we need to listen to his word.

1. Have I ever experienced "my heart burning within me" when I read Scripture or heard it proclaimed from the pulpit? If so, what was the impact of this experience on my life? *(53-55)*

2. "The fundamental attitude that we must bring to Scripture is an open heart: an eagerness to listen to the word of God and a willingness to heed it" *(57)*. To what extent is this my attitude when I sit down to read the Bible? *("Attitudes," 55-59)*

3. Do I believe that God really does want to speak to me through his word in Scripture? What does his wanting to speak to me say about my value in his eyes?

4. "What I am reading is written to me." Was this my attitude the last time I read a passage from the Bible? Did what I read apply to me as if it had been written particularly to and for me? *("Approaches," 60-64)*

5. "What I am reading is written about me." Do I identify in a special way with any of the people I read about in Scripture? Am I able to take what happened to them as a lesson and example for me?

6. To what extent have I already experienced God speaking to me through the words of Scripture? Have I ever had an experience like St. Augustine's, when a particular Scripture passage bore personal meaning for me? *("God Speaks to Us," 64-69)*

7. What is God saying to me now—or what has he said to me recently—through the words of Scripture?

8. Am I aware of the activity of the Holy Spirit in my life? How have I experienced his graces and promptings? How often do I pray to the Holy Spirit for guidance? *("The Holy Spirit," 69-76)*

9. In this section, four ways (printed in italics) are suggested in which the

Holy Spirit aids us in our Scripture reading. In which of these ways has the Holy Spirit helped me to read Scripture as God's word to me?

10. Has the Bible become "words of life" for me, or is it simply a book I find interesting? *("Words of Life," 76-79)*

11. Do I yearn for, and pray for, God to speak words of life to me?

In conclusion: Take and read. Read and listen. Listen and hear God's word to you.

Chapter Four
Praying

In summary: Reading Scripture forms a good springboard to prayer.

1. Do I have favorite biblical scenes or events that I "ponder in my heart"? What insights have I received from my pondering? Did such insights provide me with a starting point for prayer? *(81-84)*

2. "Being in the presence of Jesus and treasuring his words in our hearts is the first step of prayer" *(83)*. Has this been true for me? How might Mary be a model for me—showing me what it means to be present with Jesus and ponder his words in my heart?

3. What prevents the word of God from penetrating more deeply into me? Have I erected any barriers to God's word? Have I remembered and nourished the words God has spoken to me, or have I forgotten them? *("Keeping the Word," 84-87)*

4. Do I feel at home in the word of God? Do I feel at home in the presence of Jesus? Am I comfortable enough in his presence to be able to talk with him in prayer?

5. How do I go about entering into the presence of God? In what ways is he most present to me? How do I deal with distractions during prayer? *("Praying with the Bible," 87-92)*

6. Have the words of Scripture been springboards to prayer for me? Do I read a passage and then pray about it, or pray as I read? What method works best for me?

7. "St. Teresa of Avila defined prayer simply as a heart-to-heart conversation with him who loves us" *(91)*. How would I characterize the way I pray?

8. What are my favorite prayers from Scripture, apart from the psalms? Do I ever meditate on their words, in order to be able to pray them better?

("Praying the Words of Scripture," 92-95)

9. Do I use the psalms as part of my prayers? Which are my favorite psalms? Why are they my favorites?

10. "The purpose of prayer is union with God." Am I consciously trying to grow in union with God? How big a role does reading Scripture play in my efforts to better know and love God? *("The Fruit of Prayer," 95-96)*

In conclusion: Read a selection from Scripture, and use this reading as the basis for a time of prayer.

Part II: The Word of God
Chapter Five
The Word of God Comes in Human Words

In summary: Just as the Word became incarnate in human flesh, so God's word is incarnate in human words in Scripture.

1. Do I have a harder time accepting the full divinity of Jesus Christ or his full humanity? What does it mean for me that Jesus was tempted in every way that I am tempted? that he was subject to all the frailties of the human condition that I am subject to? *(99-102)*

2. Do I have a harder time believing that Scripture is the inspired word of God or that the words of Scripture, even though inspired, are fully human words? Would I be upset if I discovered that a biblical writer began a sentence but interrupted himself with another thought and didn't properly finish the sentence? that a biblical writer used bad grammar? that a biblical writer used a vulgar expression? (Note: Examples of these can all be found in the original Hebrew or Greek texts of the Bible but are usually smoothed over in English translations.)

3. The books of the Bible were written over a period of a thousand years, in some cases incorporating material that had already been handed on by word of mouth for centuries. Does this have implications for how I go about understanding these books? What might be some of these implications? *("The Word in History," 102-7)*

4. "The people of God were the context for the word of God to be spoken" *(107)*. How does this help me better understand the historical books of the Bible? the prophetic books?

5. Read 2 Maccabees, chapter 15, verses 37 and 38. What does verse 38 reveal about the attitude of the author? Can the Holy Spirit inspire and

guide someone without that person being aware of it? (*"The Word Becomes Words,"* 107-13)

6. Does realizing that some of the biblical books were shaped by a variety of authors and editors over the course of many decades change my view of Scripture? Do I think of the Bible as the written heritage of a people or as simply a work produced by individual inspired authors? Does this distinction make any difference in how I go about reading the Bible as God's word?

7. Do I think of the Bible as a book or as an entire library of books? I expect to find many different kinds of books in a public library, from do-it-yourself manuals to novels to history books: am I surprised that the library-that-is-the-Bible also contains many different kinds of books? What does this variety imply about how I go about understanding the Bible?

8. Does learning about the process through which the Bible came to be help me understand it better? Does its long process of development say anything to me about the way God has chosen to communicate with us through Scripture? (*"Our Bible Comes to Be,"* 113-16)

9. Do I accept that God speaks to us in fully human words in the Bible, just as the Word became fully human in Jesus of Nazareth? What are some of the implications of this for how I go about understanding the Bible as God's word? (*"The Word of God in Human Words,"* 116-18)

In conclusion: God has spoken to us in human language.

Chapter Six
It Is God Who Speaks

In summary: "It pleased God, in his goodness and wisdom, to reveal himself" (Vatican II, Divine Revelation, #2).

1. How much of the Old Testament have I read in the course of my life? What portions of it have the most appeal and meaning for me? What portions do I find difficult to understand? What are the most important lessons I have learned from the Old Testament? (*119-23*)

2. "Jesus brought to completion the teaching of the Old Testament" (*121*). When some Old Testament teaching puzzles me, do I try to

recall or search out what Jesus had to say on the topic? Do I try to interpret what I read in the Old Testament in light of Jesus?

3. What do I live for? What are my ultimate hopes? How firm is my faith
that Jesus Christ offers me resurrection to eternal life? How often do I
think about the eternal life Jesus offers me? How thoroughly does my
hope of eternal life shape my life here and now? (*"The Word of Life,"*
123-26)

4. "The basic revelation that comes through Scripture is the revelation of
God himself" (*125*). How has God made himself known to me? What
role is reading Scripture playing in my coming to know God better?
How have I encountered God in Scripture this week?

5. What is God like for me? What is my image of God? What is the significance of Jesus' calling God his Father? What is the significance of Jesus'
calling God our Father and authorizing us to pray to God as our
Father? (*"Abba,"* 126-29)

6. Jesus said, "Whoever has seen me has seen the Father" (Jn 14:9). What
does God look like seen through the window of Jesus? How would I
characterize God, if God is revealed in Jesus?

7. What does it mean for me to follow Jesus as his disciple? What does he
require of me? Where is he leading me? (*"The Way, the Truth, the Life,"*
129-33)

8. Which of Jesus' many miracles and acts of mercy most appeals to me?
Why? What does it reveal about Jesus? What does it reveal about the
one who sent him?

9. Jesus said, "As I have loved you, so you also should love one another"
(John 13:34). How has Jesus loved me? How does Jesus ask me to
love?

10. What is my image of the Holy Spirit? What kind of relationship do I
have with the Holy Spirit? What role does he play in my spiritual life?
What role should he play in my reading of Scripture? Have I ever been
conscious of receiving his help as I read the Bible? (*"The Spirit of God,"*
133-36)

In conclusion: Reach out and be touched by Someone!

Chapter Seven
It Is the Church Who Listens

In summary: Church, Scripture, and Holy Spirit are inextricably linked.

1. What is my experience of belonging to the Church? Is it a once-a-week activity for me or something more? What link do I see between being a disciple of Jesus and being a member of the Church? *(137-39)*

2. If I wanted to leave a lasting imprint on the world, how would I go about it? What means are at my disposal to leave at least a little imprint? If I were to die tonight, what imprint would I leave behind? (*"The Plan of Jesus,"* 139-42)

3. What are the implications for me of Jesus choosing rather ordinary women and men to be his first followers and to form the seed of his Church? If Jesus had come today, might he choose me to be one of his followers? What response would I make to him?

4. Jesus didn't write a book or ask anyone to transcribe his teachings, although he could have easily done so. What does this say to me about Jesus' priorities during his public ministry?

5. The first generations of Christians handed on the message of Jesus by word of mouth. Do I also try to hand on the saving message of Jesus Christ to others by what I say to them? (*"The Handing On,"* 142-48)

6. The four Gospels are edited versions of the gospel message as it was passed on by word of mouth in the early Church. How should this influence the way in which I read and understand the Gospels?

7. How important was the role of the Holy Spirit in the early Church? How important is his role in the Church today? How important a role does the Holy Spirit play in my life? How has the Spirit gifted me to serve the Church? Am I making full use of the gifts and talents I have been given? (*"The Spirit's Guidance,"* 148-53)

8. Which is truer: the Church created the Bible, or the Bible created the Church? What are the implications of this for how I read and interpret the Bible?

9. Reflect on the obvious but often overlooked fact that the Bible we read did not exist in the early days of the Church (that is, the books of the New Testament were still in the process of being written and collected

together). What would your Christian life have been like if you had lived then? What would have shaped and nourished your faith? ("*It is the Church Who Listens,*" 153-58)

10. "The Church is the place where we listen to the word of God" (*154*). How true is this for me? Would my understanding of Scripture be different if I was not a member of the Church?

In conclusion: Read Scripture as a *we* as well as an *I*: We the Church listen for God's word.

Part III: Abiding in the Word
Chapter Eight
As You Continue Reading

In summary: Various practical considerations for Bible readers.

1. Have I come across sections of the Bible that puzzled me? bored me? angered me? What are my favorite sections of the Bible? my least favorite? What parts of the Bible am I least familiar with? What is the best balance for me between drawing nourishment from the portions of the Bible I find most nourishing and yet not completely neglecting the portions I find difficult to understand and apply? ("*The Variety of Scripture,*" 161-64)

2. Have I ever read the Bible out loud to myself? Was it helpful or unhelpful for me to do so? Suggestion: Select a psalm and read it aloud as a part of your prayers today.

3. If I find myself reading a Scripture passage I do not understand, how do I react? What do I do? How well does it work? Might the three suggestions on pages 164-65 be of help to me? ("*Difficulties in Reading Scripture,*" 164-66)

4. "We read the Bible for what we can understand of it, not for what we cannot understand" (*166*). Do I let perplexities distract me from the meaning I can understand? Do I let uncertainties excuse me from putting into practice what is certain?

5. Are there particular biblical verses that have special meaning for me? What are some of these verses? How did I first come across them? What gives them their special meaning for me? ("*Special Verses,*" 166-68)

6. Do I find memorizing easy or difficult? Are there passages of Scripture that I can repeat from memory? How has having these passages readily at hand been of help to me? Do I have other favorite biblical passages that it would be helpful for me to memorize?

7. Am I, or have I been, a part of a Bible sharing group or other small sharing group? How has being a member of the group benefited me? What do I like about group sharing? What do I find difficult? (*"Small Group Sharing,"* 168-71)

8. If I am not part of a Bible sharing group, how might being in such a group be of help to me in reading, understanding, and applying the words of Scripture? Is there a group I could join? Could I form a new group with some of my friends?

In conclusion: Continue abiding in the variety of God's word,
in the variety of ways you can do so.

Chapter Nine
Some Problems of Interpretation

In summary: Consumer warning! The questions are tougher in this chapter.

1. "In Paul's letters there are some things that are hard to understand" (2 Pt 3:16). Should I be surprised if there are portions of the Bible I have trouble understanding? if there are questions about the Bible I cannot answer? (*173-75*)

2. Do I worry about an erosion of faith among Christians today? Do I worry that my own faith is becoming less sure? Do I have more doubts and perplexities than I used to? Can doubts and perplexities be occasions for me to grow in faith?

3. Do I get uneasy when people talk about human evolution or about humanlike ancestors living hundreds of thousands of years ago? How have I reconciled in my own mind what I read in the opening chapters of Genesis with current scientific theories? Or do I try to ignore any potential conflict between them? (*"Genesis 1-11,"* 175-80)

4. "The origin of the first eleven chapters of Genesis must be found in the stories of creation that were common in the Near East at the time that the contents of Genesis were evolving" (*178*). Do I find this upsetting?

Do I accept that the Holy Spirit could have inspired biblical authors to make use of old stories in order to convey truths about God's relationship with the world?

5. What kind of truths can be found in the opening chapters of Genesis? What kind of information cannot be found there? What is the message of these chapters for me?

6. Have I been bothered by apparent discrepancies between the Gospels and wondered what "really happened"? Do I attempt to arrive at a life of Jesus by adding together bits from each of the Gospels, smoothing over inconsistencies of sequence and detail? Do I take the words of Jesus in the Gospels to be a transcript of his exact words? What are the advantages and the drawbacks of the way I go about understanding the four Gospels? (*"The Gospels,"* 180-86)

7. "The truth of a story is not at all affected by the fact that the evangelists relate the words and deeds of the Lord in a different order, or express his sayings not literally but differently, while preserving their sense" (Pontifical Biblical Commission, Instruction on the Historical Truth of the Gospels, 1964). Review the three stages in the formation of the Gospels on pages 181-84. What are the implications of the Gospels being the result of this three-stage process for the way I go about understanding the Gospels?

8. "Jesus did many other signs in the presence of his disciples that are not written in this book. But these are written that you may come to believe that Jesus is the Messiah, the Son of God, and that through this belief you may have life in his name" (Jn 20:30-31, NAB). What does this tell me about the proper way to read the Gospel of John? the proper way to read all Scripture?

9. How much of the Book of Revelation have I read? How much sense did I make of what I read? Did I read it as a "tract for its times," written "to encourage Christians in the midst of persecution" (*187*)? Or did I read it as a timetable for what will happen when the world comes to an end? (*"The Book of Revelation,"* 186-89)

10. Am I frustrated that there are questions that the Bible does not clearly answer? What are some of these questions for me? What can I learn

from the silence of the Bible? Might growing in reading Scripture entail growing in acceptance of the silence of God as well as acceptance of the word of God? (*"The Silence of the Scriptures,"* 189-91)

In conclusion: We must listen to God as he has chosen to speak to us.

Chapter Ten
The Power of the Word

In summary: God's word can change us and give us life.

1. How have I experienced the power of God's word? What has been the effect of God's word in Scripture on my life? Do I read Scripture expecting God's grace to change me through its words? Do I come to Jesus as the one who alone has "words of eternal life" (Jn 6:68)? (*193*)

2. Paul commended the Christians of Ephesus to God and to "that gracious word of his that can build you up and give you your inheritance" (Acts 20:32, NAB). Have I experienced God's word as a gracious and loving word? How has God built me up through his word? How is his word drawing me toward my inheritance? (*"Conclusion,"* 199-201)

3. Am I firmly resolved to remain faithful to reading God's word in Scripture?

In conclusion: Be faithful in reading Scripture as the word of God.